THE AFTERLIFE REVEALED

WHAT HAPPENS AFTER WE DIE

THE AFTERLIFE REVEALED

WHAT HAPPENS AFTER WE DIE

BY

MICHAEL TYMN

The Afterlife Revealed

What Happens After We die

Copyright © 2011 by Michael E. Tymn. All rights reserved.

Published and printed in the United States of America and the United Kingdom
by White Crow Books; an imprint of White Crow Productions Ltd.

For information, contact White Crow Books at P. O. Box 1013 Guildford,
GU1 9EJ United Kingdom, or e-mail to info@whitecrowbooks.com.

Cover designed by Butterflyeffect
Book designed by Perseus Design
Produced by essentialworks.co.uk

Paperback ISBN 978-1-907661-90-7
eBook ISBN 978-1-907661-91-4

New Age/Metaphysical/Religion

Published by White Crow Books
www.whitecrowbooks.com

CONTENTS

An asterisk (*) following a person's name in the text indicates that the person is further identified in Appendix D.

A man should be able to say he has done his best to form a conception of life after death, or to create some image of it – even if he must confess his failure. Not to have done so is a vital loss.

— C. G. Jung

FOREWORD

Michael Tymn is one of the world's foremost living experts on afterlife studies. His earlier book *The Articulate Dead,* a study of apparent spirit accounts reaching us through mediums, presented evidence in support of the "spirit hypothesis." He concluded that the best of these accounts could not have been inventions of the subconscious mind of the medium, for they contain a great deal of information, later confirmed to be true, unknown to the medium. But this same information was well known, in earth life, to the person whose spirit was said to be communicating *through* the medium. Tymn is a master of this "evidential" approach used to evaluate spirit communications. There is perhaps no one living today who has dissected so many of them and argued so successfully for their authenticity. This method of analysis, it seems to me, makes it close to certain that we survive our physical death and enter another world as "spirits" with memories, personality, and character intact.

In this new book Tymn takes the next step. It is one thing to argue for the reality of life after death, but quite another to picture it. That is exactly what Tymn does here. Quite a bit of the book is taken up with repeating the earlier arguments for survival of death – and that is a strength of the present book – but then he ventures farther out. If you are wondering how an earthling can go about this, the answer is obvious on second thought. If we can show that a spirit communicating to us through a medium accurately recalls detailed information that his loved ones and friends later confirm, then there is good reason to take him at his word when he describes his experiences on the Other Side. If only a few "spirits" were capable of such feats, we would be wise to be on our guard. But when hundreds of voices, even thousands, coming to us through mediums from all over the world repeat much the same story, we should be impressed. What makes Tymn stand out among afterlife researchers is his perhaps uniquely vast knowledge of mediumistic sources. It is hard to believe that these sources, when assembled and collated, reveal nothing more than an enchanting chimera.

As a result, you are likely to come away from reading this book feeling that you have at least a general idea of what to expect when you die. And that can be quite sobering, as Tymn intends it to be. Nothing stands out with greater clarity than this: We – all of us – are accountable for what we do on earth, for better or worse. The justice that we all seek in this world, but seldom find as we would like it, at last has its day. The universe revealed by spirits comes across as a vast moral gymnasium, with character development, or "soul growth," the Creator's top priority. How this all works out, and the otherworldly settings for its evolution, are the focus of this fascinating book.

But this is not a book only about the afterlife. If you want to know what is expected of you *in this life,* then you would be wise to consult those intelligences closer to the Divine Source than we are. They are far from infallible, as they admit, but their point of view is inspiring and revitalizing. To anyone clueless about what life expects of us or horrified by the thought of death, this book could be life-changing *here and now.*

Abraham Lincoln worked relentlessly to show young America that democracy at its best far surpassed any other form of government that the world had seen. His aim was to spread human happiness among the masses – former slaves, immigrants, Catholics, Jews. The spirits surveyed here are inspired by something similar. They hope, from their superior vantage point, to guide the great mass of drifting, purposeless humanity toward a goal worthy of their native splendor. Ever since I have known him, Michael Tymn has regretted that the wisdom of the spirits seemed to have been lost to the world. This book is his humble gift to it. May you be helped to discover your native splendor within its pages.

Stafford Betty, Ph.D.
Professor of Religious Studies
California State University, Bakersfield
Author of *The Afterlife Unveiled*

PREFACE

LIVING IN ETERNITY

*When a man is seventy-five he cannot help some-
times thinking about death. The thought of it
leaves me perfectly calm, for I am convinced that
our spirit is absolutely indestructible...it is like
the sun which only seems to sink and in reality
never sinks at all.*

— Goethe

s I complete this book by fine-tuning the rough draft and rewrit-
ing the first paragraph of this Preface, I am into my 75th year and
currently afflicted with a mysterious blood clot in my right leg
– one that, I'm told, could fragment and travel to my heart, lungs, or
brain, ending my life. I'm in no particular hurry to leave this realm of
existence and am very much concerned about leaving my wife alone.
I'm also concerned about the possibility of surviving a stroke with di-
minished capacities. Nor does the pain connected with an embolism,
heart attack, or stroke particularly appeal to me. But, all those concerns
aside, I think I can honestly say I do not significantly fear the idea of
death itself. In fact, I find it somewhat exciting.

Many friends and relatives who know of my interest in death and afterlife research express concern that it is an unhealthy or taboo subject

matter. "One life at a time for me" is a typical reaction, a subtle and supposedly "intelligent" way of saying that the person is not interested in discussing anything related to death.

I respond to that comment by saying that I agree that we should be living in the present, not looking ahead to some distant afterlife. But I add that the best way to live in the present, or in the "now," or in the "moment," is to "live in eternity." That always brings puzzled expressions and requires some explanation. I begin by calling upon some great thinkers. As examples, the eminent Swiss psychiatrist Carl Jung said that it is psychologically beneficial to have death as a goal toward which to strive. Mozart called death the key to unlocking the door to true happiness. Shakespeare wrote that when we are prepared for death, life is sweeter. The French philosopher Michel de Montaigne said that "to practice death is to practice freedom." Essentially, what they all say is that in understanding death, in embracing death, we come to understand life and better enjoy it.

Still, my friends and relatives don't get it. Their puzzled expressions persist. It is not easy to explain how to "live in eternity," but the analogy I find best explains it is retirement from the work force. Most people, even those who find some joy and fulfillment in their jobs, look forward to retirement. They envision more freedom and opportunity to pursue things that really interest them and which involve less stress and conflict than their occupations. They anticipate more time for leisure activities, travel, maybe even an around-the-world cruise. Retirement is not something they constantly dwell on, but it is a motivator that more or less straddles the dividing line between the conscious and the subconscious. That's what "living in eternity" is like – having that long range goal in the back of the mind while still focusing on the present. It's like a baseball player taking each game as it comes, but still envisioning some day being in the Hall of Fame. It's something of a dream that continually inspires him to face up to the challenges.

"We can live with the consciousness of immortality, and it will give an added coloring and beauty to life," is the way philosopher Alice Bailey put it. "We can foster the awareness of our future transition, and live with the expectation of its wonder. Death thus faced, and regarded as a prelude to further living experience, takes on a different meaning." [1]

A group of entities, dubbed the "Invisibles" by popular author Stewart Edward White, communicated through the mediumship of White's wife, Betty. They referred to the desired awareness of spiritual matters, including death, as "habitual spiritual consciousness." Concerned that

White might misunderstand and assume that they were saying that the focus should be entirely on the spiritual world, they explained: "This does not imply any retirement into some state of permanent abstraction, nor any priggish watchfulness to determine that your every move is transcendental. It means simply that each day, when you finish your practice, you do not close the experience like a book, but carry it around with you like a treasured possession. Instead of being completely forgotten, it remains in the back of your mind, communicating its influence automatically to your actions and reactions, and ready at any moment, if specifically called upon, to lend a helping hand."[2]

The Invisibles called "balancing" the earthly life with the immortal life the "art of life." They stressed that one must be able to deal with life's adversities by viewing them from the higher consciousness.

Frederic W. H. Myers*, a Cambridge scholar and one of the founders of the Society for Psychical Research in London, is a good example of someone who was able to develop his spiritual consciousness to the point where, in embracing death, he found joy and fulfillment in life. At Myers's memorial service in 1901, Sir Oliver Lodge* recalled that Myers, when visiting the United States a few years earlier, swam the Niagara River below the treacherous falls. Myers told Lodge that the thought suddenly flashed upon him that he might die, but there was no fear connected with this thought. Rather, he saw the whole experience as a joyous adventure, for, as Lodge put it, "his clear and happy faith was the outcome entirely of his scientific researches" which strongly pointed to survival.[3]

Present at Myers's deathbed, Professor William James of Harvard wrote that "his serenity, in fact, his eagerness to go, and his extraordinary intellectual vitality up to the very time the death agony began, and even in the midst of it, were a superb spectacle and deeply impressed the doctors, as well as ourselves."[4]

But what if retirement meant no income of any kind – no savings, no social security, no pensions? There would be nothing to look forward to except poverty, squalor and despair. Unfortunately, that is how most people now look at death and the afterlife. Orthodox religion has not been able to paint a picture that offers anything more than a humdrum heaven or horrific hell. Assuming that a person feels qualified for heaven, how can he or she get excited about floating around on clouds all day while strumming a harp, or in what seems like an endless Sunday church service singing hymns and praising God? How appealing is that?

In effect, there are three approaches to viewing death: 1) a march into an abyss of nothingness; 2) seeing the humdrum heaven and horrific hell of orthodoxy; 3) viewing it like *beginning* retirement with an around-the-world cruise.

The few who embrace death see the wisdom of choosing number three. The atheists or non-believers, who make up 10-20 percent of the population in the United States and as much as 50 percent in other Western countries, stoically accept number one. Thus, the majority of people in the United States and roughly half in other Western countries mindlessly opt for number two. The problem is that they don't really "believe" in an afterlife. They just "hope" for it while striving to be "one with their toys," worshipping celebrities as gods, living completely in the moment, and having no conception of what death brings. In effect, materialism is their philosophy.

Clearly, the philosophy of materialism has resulted in an era of moral decadence, a time of egocentricity, intolerance, hatred, hypocrisy, disorder, flux, strife, chaos, and fear. We have become hedonistic materialists, consumed with the pursuit of pleasure and sensory gratification, making merry with intoxicants and drugs, and reveling in the "Playboy" philosophy. In fact, *Playboy* magazine founder Hugh Heffner is often portrayed in the media as a great success story, even a role model for many.

I was reminded of our changing values not long ago while listening to four high school seniors vying for the title of homecoming queen. I was asked to serve as a judge of their 10-minute talks on the subject of "heroes."

One of contestants said that her heroes were all those people who helped her "have fun." I don't know if the applause that followed was out of politeness or whether the audience actually agreed with her. It seems obvious, however, that a majority of today's young people are more focused on "having fun" than on establishing meaningful goals, much more so than was the case with prior generations.

Two of the other contestants chose movie actresses, while the fourth chose an athlete. Since movie actors are simply people pretending to be people and, given the fact that sports grew out of practice for war, athletes are pretend combatants, it seems increasingly clear that we have lost touch with reality. The unreal has become the real.

Popular author Philip Yancey states that the seven deadly sins might today be renamed the seven seductive virtues. The truth of his statement is evident when we stop to recognize how *greed* and *envy* drive our economy, how *anger* fuels terrorism, how *lust* is openly celebrated on television, how athletes and other entertainers go far beyond *pride*, arrogantly flaunting their prowess with various forms of exhibitionism. One has to have his head buried in the sand to not see how *gluttony* and *sloth* are rampant in our country.

In his 1988 commencement address to Cornell University graduates, Dr. Frank Rhodes, then president of Cornell, addressed the problem relative to science, pointing out that its reductionist thinking has been adopted by academia and has resulted in abstraction, detachment, moral abstention, and depersonalization. Consequently, he told graduating seniors, setting meaningful goals will be difficult.

More recently, in a 2003 keynote address at a University of Buffalo conference on "Fostering Ultimate Meaning," Dr. Alexander Astin, Director of the Higher Education Research Institute at the University of California at Los Angeles, said that developing a meaningful philosophy of life was the top value for college students in the 1970s, but that students today are more focused on material gain. He attributed the value shift to the growing influence of television.

Can any thinking person doubt that today's hedonistic materialism is a result of a loss of spiritual values, especially a lack of belief in the survival of consciousness after death? Can there be any other reason for it?

After Betty White died in 1939, she began communicating with her husband, Stewart Edward White, through the trance mediumship of a woman known only as "Joan," as she preferred to remain anonymous. One of the most popular books of the era, *The Unobstructed Universe*, authored by Stewart Edward White, set forth the discoveries of Betty White after her death. One of the first things Betty mentioned was the collapse of the "old order of things." When Stewart asked her what had brought about the collapse, she bluntly responded: "Loss of faith in the present fact of immortality."

Betty explained that she was not referring to a conscious attitude of agnosticism or denial. "We may still profess belief in a vague and remote 'heaven' to which eventually we shall go," she said through Joan's vocal cords. "But belief is not faith; and it is only *faith* – faith in the same sense that we accept the inevitability of death itself – that can transfer the field of our practical endeavor out of the present moment. When the present moment – the earth span of life – is all that concerns us, then the emphasis of all we think and all we do at once bases on materialism." [5]

In his 1974 Pulitzer prize-winning book, *The Denial of Death*, cultural anthropologist Ernest Becker pointed out that death anxiety is at the root of all human activity. "The idea of death, the fear of it, haunts the human animal like nothing else," Becker wrote. "It is a mainspring of human activity - activity designed largely to avoid the fatality of death, to overcome it by denying it in some way that it is the final destiny of man." [6]

To free oneself of death anxiety, Becker explained, nearly everyone chooses the path of repression. We bury the anxiety deep in the subconscious and go about our everyday activities mostly oblivious to the fact that in the great scheme of things those activities are exceedingly short-term and for the most part meaningless.

As Becker saw it, basic repression is the enemy of mankind. The theme of his book is that the unrepressed life can bring into birth a new man. In another book along the same line, *The Broken Connection*, Robert Jay Lifton, a distinguished professor of psychiatry and psychology, says much the same thing as Becker – that we must "know death" in order to live with free imagination.

Lifton tells us that we have to be able to imagine it, to visualize it before we can accept the survival of consciousness. Therein is the failure of orthodox religion; there is nothing to visualize beyond those harps and clouds. When we truly embrace death, we can begin to visualize something, even though it may never be completely in focus. In so visualizing, we begin to comprehend the divine plan. We are able to understand that there is no sudden enlightenment on the "other side." There is no heaven-hell dichotomy. Rather, there are planes or dimensions to which our undying minds or souls gravitate based on the spiritual development achieved on earth. We are able to formulate a paradigm that involves a Creative Force, whatever shape He, She, or It takes, and are able to see how the divine plan plays itself out in cosmic evolution. We see how we are really souls occupying bodies rather than bodies housing souls and how our souls are progressing in finding their way back to Oneness with the Creator through the challenges, the adversities, the trials and tribulations offered us in a particular lifetime. We understand how a life without adversity offers little opportunity for growth. We come to appreciate the words of Mozart that "death, as we consider it closely, is the true goal of our existence."

As Jung viewed it, the decisive question for man is whether he is related to something infinite or not. "That is the telling question of his life," Jung declared. "Only if we know that the thing which truly matters is the infinite can we avoid fixing our interest upon futilities, and upon all kinds of goals which are not of real importance." [7]

Existentialist philosopher Søren Kierkegaard wrote: "If there were no eternal consciousness in a man, if at the foundation of all there lay only a wildly seething power which writhing with obscure passions produced everything that is great and everything that is insignificant, if a bottomless void never satiated lay hidden beneath all – what then would life be but despair?" [8]

Kierkegaard called "Philistinism" the worst kind of despair. The Philistine, as Kierkegaard saw him, is someone so tranquilized in the mundane or the trivial that he lacks the awareness that he is even in despair. "For Philistinism thinks it is in control of possibility, it thinks that when it has decoyed this prodigious elasticity into the field of probability or into the mad-house it holds it a prisoner; it carries possibility around like a prisoner in the cage of the probable, shows it off, imagines itself to be the master, does not take note that precisely thereby it has taken itself captive to be the slave of spiritlessness and to be the most pitiful of all things...but philistinism spiritlessly celebrates its triumph." [9]

William James, one of the pioneers of psychology, alluded to the philosophy of "living in the moment" when he said that "the luster of the present hour is always borrowed from the background of possibilities it goes with." [10] In other words, you can't effectively live in the present without considering the future. Of course, age is a factor in this regard, the younger person finding it easier to "seize the day." James went on to say that a nameless *Unheimlichkeit*, i.e., eeriness, comes over us at the thought of there being nothing eternal in our final purpose, in the objects of those loves and aspirations which are our deepest energies.

The bottom line here, for those accepting the reasoning of Jung, Kierkegaard, and James, as I do, is that it is impossible for a thinking person to find *true purpose* in life without a belief in survival – limited, restricted, and temporal purpose, perhaps, but not *true* purpose. This belief must go beyond the blind or pseudo-faith of most religious practitioners. It must take the form of *conviction*. "Too many indeed hold the solemn verities concerning the hereafter in a sort of half consciousness, believing in them, yet nevertheless not fully realizing them," wrote Dr. Madison Peters, a Christian author of a century ago. "They must flame within us, setting our whole moral and intellectual nature on fire, sending a life current of energy though every part of our being, arousing us to impetuous action and to sustained effort born of strong conviction." [11]

Not only is the fear of death overcome by embracing it, but once we fully cultivate an awareness of the larger life and internalize it, we are better able to put the spiritual back in balance with the material and experience a life of love and service. We unlock the door to true happiness – happiness not dependent on material wealth.

Addressing concerns that being too focused on the afterlife will make a person unfit for the "practical" life, philosopher Lilian Whiting pointed out that the truth is just the opposite. "Let one realize the absolute continuity of existence and at once life becomes worth living," she offered.[12]

Yes, it *is* possible to view death in a positive light, in the same way we view retirement, but, unfortunately, orthodox religion has been as closed-minded as mainstream science in opening itself to true enlightenment. The Bible tells us to "seek and ye shall find," and further says that "seek ye first the kingdom of God." But you have to know where to look, and orthodox religion is content to grope in the darkness.

In writing this book, I am hoping that at least a few people might read it and begin to visualize a spirit world, thereby helping them make friends with death, at the same time making this life more meaningful. But there is another reason. Many spirit messages suggest that knowledge of fundamental facts about the way things work on the "other side" facilitates one's "awakening" and progress in the new environment.

[1] Bailey, Alice A., *Death: The Great Adventure*, Lucis Press Ltd., London, 1985, p.2

[2] White, Stewart Edward, *Across the Unknown*, Ariel Press, Columbus, OH, 1987, p. 155

[3] Eddy, Sherwood, *You Will Survive Death*, The Omega Press, Surrey, UK, 1954, p. 45

[4] Hamilton, Trevor, *Immortal Longings*, Imprint-Academic.com, Exeter,UK, 2009, p. 274

[5] White, Stewart Edward, *The Unobstructed Universe*, E. P. Dutton & Co., New York, 1940, p. 35

[6] Becker, Ernest, *The Denial of Death*, Simon & Schuster, NY, 1973, Preface xvii

[7] Jung, C. G., *Memories, Dreams, Reflections*, Vintage Books, NY, 1961, p. 325

[8] Kierkegaard, S., *Fear and Trembling*, Doubleday & Co., Garden City, NY, 1954, p 30

[9] _____pp. 174-175

[10] James, William, "The Varieties of Religious Experience," 1902, p. 124

[11] Peters, Madison C., D.D., *After Death What?* The Christian Herald, 1908, p. 87

[12] Whiting, Lilian, *The Spiritual Significance*, Little, Brown, & Co., Boston, 1901, p. 127

INTRODUCTION

REVELATION: ANCIENT VS. MODERN

I have much more to say to you, more than you can now bear. But when he, the Spirit of truth, comes, he will guide you into all the truth. He will not speak on his own; he will speak only what he hears, and he will tell you what is yet to come.
John 16: 12-14

Although I had watched the ABC TV 20/20 special, *Heaven - Where Is It? How Do We Get There?* when it aired a year or so earlier, I forgot how bad it was and ended up watching the rerun. I had a very difficult time enduring the interviews with various religious leaders, especially the evangelical, whatever his name was, and I would have changed channels were it not for the fact that I knew there would be a few near-death experiencers (NDErs) offering testimony. I could not remember what they had to say and was a little curious. I also forgot that the 20/20 people presented a biased view of the NDE by allowing a debunker to say that the near-death experience is nothing more than the imaginings of a dying brain, while not offering the testimony of one of many credible scientific researchers prepared to counter such a statement.

Unfortunately, the NDErs came at the end and so I struggled through the preceding hour and 40 minutes of the two-hour program. Had I had been a skeptic beforehand, I would no longer be a skeptic. I would be a total disbeliever. The religious leaders, including the evangelical, a Catholic priest, a Jewish rabbi, an Islamic scholar, and the Dalai Lama offered no enlightenment. They simply gave their versions of what ancient books and tradition had to say about a dichotomous afterlife, i.e., the old Heaven and Hell stuff. The Catholic priest made no mention of Purgatory and the Dalai Lama did not define "Heaven" or go beyond what he saw as the highest state. Of course, they all painted rosy pictures of Heaven, pretty humdrum nevertheless.

Host and interviewer Barbara Walters ignorantly approached the whole subject with the assumption that 1) there is a "Heaven" and a "Hell," as taught by orthodoxy, or 2) there is "nothingness," as the atheist on the panel was so certain of. One was left to conclude from the testimony of the religious leaders that we end our earthly lives being labeled as either "righteous" or "wicked" – no in-between – and our environment is then either positive or negative – Heaven or Hell.

In the blissful state of heaven, we should find, according to some religions, souls who led selfish and hateful lives but who repented on their deathbeds along with other wicked souls who "found" their savior just before dying and suddenly became righteous. Among the tormented, we should expect to find souls who led righteous lives for most of their years but who transgressed just before dying or did not choose the right savior. It is difficult to reconcile much of this with the loving, forgiving and just God they see as governing that afterlife. Indeed, their God often appears cruel, capricious, vindictive, jealous, and wrathful. The "religious" respond to such a charge by saying that God's ways are beyond our comprehension, and we should not attempt to apply our own standards of justice to something we are incapable of understanding. What a copout!

All of those so-called leaders, except possibly for the Dalai Lama, are clearly locked into ancient beliefs because they accept translations which suggest that revelation ended with whatever old book or books they subscribe to. Any revelation since those books were closed is rejected as fraudulent or inspired by the devil. They disregard the fact that their books have so many parables, so many metaphors, so many similes, so many allegories, so many translations, so many interpretations, so many elucidations of ancient writings that the subject matter lends itself to a semantical maze or nightmare.

Our search for the origins of the Jewish and Christian afterlife beliefs begins in the Old Testament with Genesis 37:35, where Jacob, upon being told that his son Joseph had been devoured by a beast, states he must go down to Sheol in mourning for his son. Exactly what Jacob meant is subject to various interpretations. The other 65 references to Sheol in the Old Testament are similarly vague, some of them suggesting that Sheol simply meant the grave while from others we can infer that it was a shadowy underworld where departed spirits roamed in a state of confusion while awaiting a final resurrection and judgment. The King James Version of the Bible translates Sheol as "Hell" 31 times, "grave" 31 times, and "pit" three times. And, yet, in Job 26:6 and Psalms 139:8, we read that the souls in Sheol still have a connection to God. In Job 14:13, Job asks God to hide him in Sheol until His anger has passed, thereby suggesting that Sheol is not a permanent abode.

In the Septuagint, the oldest Greek version of the Old Testament, Sheol becomes Hades, although Hades is also used in several places to mean other things. In ancient Greek mythology, Hades was also an intermediate state for souls. From there, the blessed would go to Elysium and all others to the infernal regions of Tartarus. "The Greeks termed this place Hades, the Egyptians the Underworld, and the Hebrews Sheol," Arthur Findlay summarizes it in *The Psychic Stream*. "These terms all meant the same place, where the dead existed till the arrival of the Saviour-Judge who would separate believers from unbelievers. The believers then went with him to Heaven while the unbelievers were consigned to Hell, a lake of fire under the earth, volcanoes being its chimneys."[1]

The traditional Jewish thought seems to be that only the very righteous go to Gan Eden (Garden of Eden). The average person goes to an intermediate state, apparently Sheol, for punishment and/or purification, while the wicked go to Gehenna, a place of eternal punishment (although some Jews see Gehenna as the intermediate state). This intermediate state is referred to by Catholics as Purgatory. Catholics point to 2 Maccabees 12:39-46, 1 Corinthians 3:11-15, Matthew 5:25-26, and 12:31-32 to support their belief in the doctrine of Purgatory. Although they do not clearly state it, these passages all suggest a realm where one purges his sins before being admitted to Heaven. A Catholic Internet source quotes St. Augustine from *The City of God*: "Temporal punishments are suffered by some in this life only, by some after death, by some both here and hereafter, but all of them before that last and strictest judgment. But not all who suffer temporal punishments after death will come to eternal punishments, which are to follow after the judgment."[2]

The Protestant Reformation attempted to do away with the idea of Purgatory. In fact, it was the primary issue giving rise to the break with the Catholic Church. Martin Luther rebelled against the corruption involved with buying indulgences to shorten one's sentence in Purgatory. Rather than attempt to make sense of it, Protestantism offered a black and white afterlife, Hell or Heaven, even though the righteous soul does not *fully* experience the bliss of Heaven until after the Resurrection and the wicked soul does not *fully* realize his punishment until that time. However, at the same time, some Protestant scholars see degrees of punishment in Hell. Pointing to Matthew 11:21-24, Dr. Robert A. Morey, a professor of Apologetics and Hermeneutics at Perry Bible Institute, states that "while all sinners in Hell will be perfectly miserable, they will not be equally miserable."[3]

According to Morey, the word *nephesh* is used 754 times in the Hebrew Bible, but it takes on 30 different meanings, ranging from "soul" and "the dead" to "fish" and "dogs," while the Greek word *aion* is found in the New Testament 108 times and is given 10 different meanings, including "forever," "ages," "occasionally," and "never." What we read in the English Bible as "everlasting punishment" meant "age-long pruning" in the original Greek. The modern English versions translate the Old Testament as saying "the dead know nothing" and that we should not be communicating with the "dead." However, it is my understanding that the original Hebrew word referred to the "spiritually dead," meaning low-level or earthbound spirits.

If the dead know nothing and we shouldn't be talking with them, why should we or how can we "test the spirits, as to whether they are of God," as we are instructed in 1 John 4:1? Why should anyone bother to "discern" what the spirits have to say, as we are counseled in 1 Corinthians 12:10, if they know nothing and we shouldn't even be communicating with them?

How are we to interpret 1 Thessalonians 5:21, which says to "test them all and hold on to what is good"? Or 1 Peter 1:5, which tells us that we should add "knowledge" to our faith?

If the Bible is to be interpreted literally, then why do Christian leaders ignore all of those Old Testament teachings, such as putting to death both persons in an adulterous relationship (Deut. 22:22), stoning to death stubborn and rebellious children (Deut. 21:18-21), accepting polygamy (Deut. 21:15), sanctioning slavery (Lev. 25:44), not eating shellfish (Lev. 11:10), or not having one's hair trimmed (Lev. 19:27)?

While religions seem to be locked into this ancient revelation, there has been, whether they recognize it or not, more recent revelation. It seems to have begun with the teachings of Emanuel Swedenborg*, the

18th Century scientist, inventor, and mystic whose clairvoyant visions and/or out-of-body travel allowed him to visit the afterlife realms. The revelation continued with the teachings of Spiritualism and Theosophy during the late 19th Century. Science jumped in with the formation of the Society for Psychical Research in London during 1882, sorting out the charlatans from the true mediums and closely examining the messages coming through the latter to determine if they were in fact originating with discarnate souls. During the 20th Century, science took on the study of past life memories and then began taking a close look at the near-death experience. There is also research going on in electronic voice phenomena, instrumental trans-communication, and induced after-death communication.

But religious leaders have for the most part rejected this new revelation. Christian leaders cite Revelation 22:18, in which John supposedly says that God will punish anyone who adds or takes away anything from the Bible. And, yet, in John 16:12-14, as set forth in the epigraph of this Introduction, we are told that there is much more to learn but the world, at least then, was not yet ready for it. Are we to assume that the world is still not ready for it and will never be ready for it?

And how are we to reconcile Joel 2:28-29, which says: "It shall come to pass afterwards that I will pour out my spirit upon all flesh; and your sons and your daughters shall prophesy, your old men shall dream dreams, your young men shall see visions, and also upon the servants and upon the handmaids in those days I will pour out my spirit."?

This more modern revelation has come to us in the same way that the ancient revelation did – through mediums of one kind or another, even though those ancient mediums, whether clairvoyants, trance types, direct voice types, automatic writers, or even near-death experiencers, might have been called prophets, seers, saints, or even saviors (or were translated as such). What the ancients called an "angel of the Lord" might now be referred to as a "spirit guide." Where it is written that "his eyes were opened and he saw a vision," might be translated today as saying the person was a clairvoyant. The method by which Moses received the Ten Commandments might today be called "direct writing" or "automatic writing."

If Christian leaders were to closely examine the newer messages, they would realize that the basic teachings of Jesus – *Love thy neighbor...*, *Do unto others...*, and *You reap what you sow* – are also the teachings emerging from the modern revelation. Moreover, many of the current messages pay homage to Jesus and suggest that he pretty much functions in what might be called "Chairman of the Board" on the Other Side. With proper testing and discernment, numerous new teachings edify and clarify Scripture, offering us language that is not muddled and befuddled by human hands and brains.

If they were to open their minds to more recent revelation, after "testing" it and "discerning" it, orthodox leaders would see a much more dynamic afterlife. As Sir Arthur Conan Doyle, the physician who created Sherlock Holmes, said, the revelations coming through spiraling mediumship during the late 19th and early 20th Century abolish the idea of an immediate grotesque hell or fantastic heaven. Rather, we come to understand that the "afterlife" is made up of a number of spheres, levels, dimensions, or planes, however they might be labeled, through which we gradually rise until reaching Oneness – a state, which, we are told, is beyond human comprehension. We also are told that we retain our individuality in this Oneness.

If, as fundamentalists believe, Scripture is the inerrant word of God (vis-à-vis the inspired word of the spirit world manipulated by man), we must conclude that God lacked in communicative skills or in the ability to foresee the confusion concerning the conflicting interpretations given to the Bible after numerous translations. "They [the ancient words of Scripture] have frequently blinded us from seeing and entering the experience they seek to describe because these words are always limited by their time, their culture, and their apprehension of reality," John Shelby Spong, a bishop of the Episcopal Church, recently wrote.[4]

Much of orthodoxy clearly interprets Scripture in a self-serving, self-stultifying way and does not grasp the fact that the foundation of the Bible is similar spirit communication coming through mediums of one kind or another. "If we were to expunge all accounts of the apparently paranormal from the pages of the Bible, we would be left with an intolerably emasculated volume," Canon (Dr.) Michael Perry of the Church of England wrote.[5]

"If you had the complete and unamended text of Christ's doctrines, many a load imposed by man in the name of religion and Christianity would be taken from your shoulders," a spirit speaking through a trance medium, a young peasant boy, told Father Johannes Greber, a Catholic priest in Germany, in 1923. "Many precepts which you are expected to believe, even though it seems out of all reason, would be discarded because it would be recognized as being wrong, and you, as God's children, could again breathe freely." The same spirit communicator previously told Greber that the teachings of Christ are no longer to be found in their original purity and clearness, that entire chapters have been omitted, and that what we now have are "mutilated copies." [6]

Was that spirit simply a "wolf in sheep's clothing," as religious leaders would no doubt claim? What can we believe? Perhaps the best guide is Matthew 7:16: "By their fruits ye shall know them." The 23rd chapter of Proverbs, seventh verse, which reads, "For as he thinketh in his heart, so is he," also offers guidance in this respect. It is difficult to read the wisdom that has come through so many credible mediums in recent centuries and believe that the spirits communicating this information are attempting to mislead us, as they offer a much more sensible and more appealing afterlife environment – one that can be reconciled with a loving and just God rather than a cruel, capricious, vindictive, and wrathful one or one who would offer a humdrum Heaven or horrific Hell. From this new revelation we discover a Divine plan – one of attainment and attunement, of gradual spiritual growth, of evolution of spirit through progressively higher (in vibration) planes.

There is so much to be found outside the highly guarded boundaries of mainstream science and orthodox religion for those willing to open their minds to it, for those willing to recognize that the dissemination of Truth did not stop with the good books of organized religion and cannot always be found in the laboratory.

If we are to overcome the sad state of affairs in the world today, science must move from cynicism to true, open-minded skepticism, seriously looking at the results of credible psychical research and parapsychology, while orthodox religion must come out of its fortress and permit its faithful to move from pseudo-faith to true faith, or conviction, by opening itself to the lessons of modern revelation. The media and corporate world must also contribute by placing morality over profit.

Unfortunately, it does not appear that the worldviews of either mainstream science or orthodox religion will significantly change in the foreseeable future. Thus, we can only hope for a gradual spiritual awakening led by scientists, theologians, and business executives who see the errors in their smug, self-serving, self-righteous, closed-minded thinking and courageously go public with their newfound views.

Only then will hedonistic materialism begin to give way to lives of hope, tolerance, patience, purpose, forbearance, kindness, love, and service.

1   Findlay, Arthur, *The Psychic Stream*, Psychic Press Ltd., London, 1939, p. 203

2   http://www.catholic.com, p. 4

3   Morey, Robert A., *Death and the Afterlife*, Bethany House Publishers, Minneapolis, MN, 1984, p. 153

4   Spong, John Shelby, *Rescuing the Bible from Fundamentalism*, HarperCollins Publishers, New York, NY, 1991, p. 245

5   Perry, Michael, Psychical and Spiritual, The Churches' Fellowship for Psychical and Spiritual Studies, Lincolnshire, 2002, p. 48

6   Greber, Johannes, *Communication with The Spirit World of God*, Johannes Greber Memorial Foundation, Teaneck, NJ, 1979, p. 20

1

THE MESSENGERS

But the manifestation of Spirit is given to every man to profit withal. For to one is given by the Spirit the word of wisdom; to another the word of knowledge by the same Spirit; to another faith by the same Spirit; to another the gift of healing by the same Spirit; to another the working of miracles; to another prophecy; to another discerning of spirits; to another divers kinds of tongues; to another the interpretation of tongues.

1 Corinthians 12:7-10

The Age of Reason, is said to have originated in the 17th century and to have been primarily an 18th-century movement, but its greatest impact was during the 19th century following Thomas Paine's book, *The Age of Reason*, published in three parts (1794, 1795, and 1807). It prompted educated people to question long-standing religious beliefs. As a result, many began rejecting God and the idea of an afterlife. The crowning blow came with Darwinism, which began with the publication of *The Origin of Species* in 1859. The latter part of the 19th century was a time of despair and hopelessness for many. "We were all in the first flush of triumphant Darwinism, when terrene evolution had explained so much that men hardly cared to look beyond," wrote Cambridge scholar and pioneering psychical researcher

Frederic W. H. Myers* in explaining why he began searching for evidence of the soul.[1]

"Never, perhaps, did man's spiritual satisfaction bear a smaller proportion to his needs," Myers further explained the mood of the day. "The old-world sustenance, however earnestly administered, [was] too unsubstantial for the modern cravings. And thus through our civilized societies two conflicting currents [ran]. On the one hand, health, intelligence, morality – all such boons as the steady progress of planetary evolution can win for the man – [were] being achieved in increasing measure. On the other hand this very sanity, this very prosperity, [brought out] in stronger relief the underlying *Weltschmerz*, the decline of any real belief in the dignity, the meaning, the endlessness of life.

"There [were] many, of course, who readily [accepted] this limitation of view; who [were] willing to let earthly activities and pleasures gradually dissipate and obscure the larger hope. But others [could not] thus be easily satisfied. They rather resemble children who are growing too old for their games – whose amusement sinks into indifference and discontent for which the fitting remedy is an initiation into the serious work of men."[2]

The seminal event giving rise to the advent of "modern" revelation occurred on March 31, 1848 just outside Rochester, New York, in the hamlet of Hydesville. Shortly after moving into a small house there on December 11, 1847, the family of John D. Fox, including daughters Margaret, 14, and Kate, 8, began hearing strange raps in the house, but it wasn't until March 31 that the two daughters realized that they could communicate with the "raps" by snapping their fingers. Upon learning of this, Mrs. Fox asked the "raps" to respond to questions by giving two raps for a "yes" and silence for "no." She asked if a human being was making the raps. There was no response. When she asked if it was a spirit, there were two raps. Neighbors were called in and dozens of questions put to the "spirit." It was determined that the spirit had been murdered in the house about five years earlier, well before the Fox family moved in, and that he had been buried beneath the house. Digging began and at a depth of five feet human remains were found.

It was soon realized that the Fox sisters were mediums and were able to bring through other spirits. Some amazing phenomena produced by their spirit controls were witnessed by a number of eminent men and women, including Horace Greeley, J. Fenimore Cooper, and William Cullen Bryant.

In spite of limited mass communications in those days, the story of the "Rochester knockings" spread rapidly and turned into an epidemic of spirit communication. Mediums began developing in all parts of the United States as well as in Europe. The phenomena progressed from rappings and tappings to table tilting and turning and table levitations. The table phenomena usually involved sitters placing their hands on the table and the table lifting off the floor, although there were many observations of the table tilting, turning, or lifting independently of any hands. The spirit communicator would then respond to the questions by tilts of the table. In addition to the simple "yes" and "no" method employed in the Fox case, spirits would tap out letters of the alphabet (one tap for "A," five taps for "E," etc.) or would respond with a tap when the alphabet was recited by someone present, thereby slowly spelling out words and sentences. The madness came to be called "Spiritualism."

If the spirits who communicated in the years immediately following the Hydesville event are to be believed, there was a plan behind it all – a plan that resulted from a growing loss of faith and spiritual values in an increasingly materialistic world. A few years before the Rochester knockings, Andrew Jackson Davis*, a young New York man, began receiving profound messages purportedly coming from high spirits, but few paid any attention to him until the epidemic was underway. Numerous books of wisdom flowed from the pen of this uneducated man, who came to be known as "the Poughkeepsie seer." Some years passed before an entry was discovered in Davis' journal for March 31. It read: "About daylight this morning a warm breathing passed over my face and I heard a voice, tender and strong, saying, 'Brother, the good work has begun – behold a living demonstration is born.' I was left wondering what could be meant by such a message." [3]

Actually, modern revelation really seems to have begun with the teachings of Emanuel Swedenborg*, a Swedish scientist, inventor, and statesman who began having mystical experiences in 1745, at age 57. He claimed that he was able to enter into "the world of spirits" and converse with them. He penned 30 volumes setting forth his discoveries. Paramount among his findings was that there was an intermediate region between heaven and hell, where spirits dwelled in much the same conditions as those on earth. It was not the purgatory of Catholicism, however, but a place where man picks up where he had left off in the material world. While Swedenborg's teachings influenced many, including Blake, Coleridge, Emerson, the Brownings, Balzac, Goethe,

Thoreau and Oliver Wendell Holmes, it was not enough to stem the tide of materialism that swept over the world during the latter part of the 19th Century.

According to spirit messages received by the Rev. William Stainton Moses* during the 1870s, the rapping method was invented by Sweden-borg and Benjamin Franklin working together in the spirit world. Moses was told that in the old days spirits communicated with men in ways less material, but as men grew more corporeal it became necessary for a material system of telegraphy to be invented. It also became increasingly clear that the communicating spirits have as many obstacles to overcome in communicating with us and we have in communicating with them.

The Spiritualism epidemic that began in Hydesville gave rise to much fraud. Even the Fox sisters, apparently under pressure to produce results on every occasion after coming under the management of showman P. T. Barnum, are said to have used tricks when the spirits were silent or unable to penetrate the veil. However, it became clear to serious investigators that much of the phenomena could not have been faked.

Like many other educated people, Dr. George T. Dexter, a New York physician, resisted the phenomena of Spiritualism. "I was positively opposed to it, and regarded the whole matter as either a foolish delusion or an absolute, outrageous deception," Dexter explained in *Spiritualism*, an 1853 book co-authored with Judge John W. Edmonds of the New York Supreme Court. However, Dexter was open-minded enough to investigate. During September 1851, he invited one of the better known mediums of the area to his house. "For the first time, I heard the peculiar sounds called spirit-raps," Dexter wrote. "I was not satisfied with the results of the sitting, though many mental questions were propounded and answered correctly." [4]

Another sitting with the same medium was arranged for the following day. After the sitting began, Dexter's nine-year-old daughter was suddenly seized by some unknown force, her arms flailing in all directions. "Her hand was made to write legibly and in bold, large letters, not in the least resembling her ordinary handwriting, full answers to all our questions, both mental and oral," Dexter explained. "And what was yet more remarkable, she wrote rapidly and easily, and the style of the composition and the spelling far excelled what we know was the character of her original attempts at composition, or her spelling, previous to this time." [5]

When his daughter showed fatigue, she was ordered by the spirits to leave the circle. When the instructions were ignored, her chair was pulled from under her by some invisible agency and she fell to the floor. "She arose to go to the next room, and as she was passing a sofa she was taken up bodily, by the same unseen force, and deposited upon it, as gently as if laid there by her parents," Dexter continued the story. "At this sitting, there were many correct answers given to questions, and of such a character as satisfied some individuals that the spirits of their friends were there." [6]

But Dexter refused to believe that spirits had anything to do with what he observed. He preferred to believe that it was some kind of mind over matter action or the power of magnetic motion. "The idea that spirits of our deceased friends could hold communion with ourselves on earth, could impart their feelings to us, give us a description of the various stages and conditions of their progress in the spheres above us, that they are constantly with those to whom they are attached, except when called away by the duties they are required to perform, that they have the power, through this new discovery, to explain to us every act of their spirit life, and receive from us the ordinary ideas which characterize our existence and connection here, was so strange, wonderful, and extraordinary, so incompatible with my education, so much opposed to all my preconceived opinions, conflicted so much with my religious belief, and with all that I had been instructed the Bible revealed to us, when compared with all I had seen at the circle, bewildered me," Dexter went on, adding that he witnessed his daughter speak "the most elevated thoughts couched in language far beyond her comprehension, describing facts in science, and circumstances in the daily life of the spirit after death." Moreover, he heard her, impromptu, recite verse after verse of poetry, "glowing with inspiration and sparkling with profound thoughts and sentiment, and yet this child never wrote a line of poetry before in her life." [7]

Dexter further witnessed phenomena with others, including an illiterate mechanic speaking Greek, Latin, Hebrew, and Chaldaic, while describing the customs and habits of men living on the earth thousands of years ago. He also observed a medium answering questions in Italian even though she knew nothing of the language.

Many of the messages were evidential. "Frequently when I have asked for evidence of identity from a spirit professing to be a near relative, the medium has repeated the same phrases and expressions, and has uttered the same words of endearment and affection that the relative was in the habit of using in his intercourse with me on earth, when by no possibility could this medium have known that I ever had such relation, or that he ever lived in this world." [8]

A short time thereafter, Dexter began to develop into a writing medium. He was sitting alone in his office late one night and leaning back in his rocking chair with his right arm resting on the arm of the chair, while concentrating on something that had nothing to do with Spiritualism. "As my hand lay on the arm of the chair I felt a singular sensation in the whole limb, as if the arm were grasped by two hands at the upper part," he recalled. "I attempted to raise it, but was unable to do so, and as soon as I made the effort to move it, the fingers were bent down tightly on the arm of the chair and grasped it firmly. Immediately the hand began to tremble, and as I watched the movement the whole limb was shaken violently. At this moment I distinctly heard two loud raps on the upper part of the side wall of the room, and it then occurred to me that his unseen power, whose manifestation I had so often witnessed, was in some way operating on me. To satisfy myself, I asked in an audible voice, 'Did the spirits just rap?' There were three distinct raps in reply. I then asked, 'Are the spirits trying to influence me?' Again, there were three distinct raps. At this I arose from my chair, arranged my books, and retired." [9]

Dexter had no desire to be influenced by spirits and resisted further attempts. He was so opposed to it that he withdrew from further sittings in his circle. "During the time I abstained from sitting in the circle, I was twice lifted bodily from my bed, moved off its edge, and thus suspended in the air," he further reported on the strange happenings. "The first time I was so dealt with, I had retired to a different room from the one I usually occupied. I had not been asleep, and was conscious of everything around me. As I lay composing myself for sleep, I discovered my whole body was slightly trembling in every fiber. I attempted to raise my hand, but I could not move; my eyes were closed, and the lids fastened. My mind was unusually active, and I noted every thing that took place with an intenseness of perception I never before experienced. My bodily sensation was likewise increased in power. As I lay there unable to move a limb, my body was lifted from the bed, and moved gently toward the edge, and with the bedclothes over it; there it remained a moment, and then it was moved off the bed into the room, suspended in the air, and there held for an instant. Just at this time the fire-bells rang an alarm, and my body was suddenly brought back to the bed and deposited in the same place I had previously occupied, with sort of a jerk, as if it had been dropped from the hands which held it." [10]

Dexter eventually gave in to the impulses. At first the sentences were short, and contained a single idea, but as he developed entire essays began coming through from spirits claiming to be Swedenborg and Francis Bacon. Judge Edmonds and several friends then began joining him in a regular circle. Over a period of several months, volumes of teachings were offered by Swedenborg and Bacon, much of which was foreign to or in conflict with what Dexter, Edmonds, and the others believed.

"I know nothing of what is written until after it is read to me, and frequently, when asked to read what has been communicated. I have found it utterly impossible to decipher it" Dexter wrote. "Not only is the thought concealed, but after it has been read to me I lose all recollection of the subject, until again my memory is refreshed by the reading. This peculiar effect on my recollection occurred more frequently when the spirits commenced writing, and I have been told by them that it was produced by their efforts to separate the action of my own mind from their thoughts, when teaching on a subject which required several sittings to finish." [11]

While other mediums were clearly being used by spirits to prove the existence of the spirit world, offering only identity and trivial bits of information, Dexter's mediumship apparently had a different objective. "It is not for the purpose of showing to the world that spirits can confer with man, or that God's law obtains in spirit-connection as well as physical," Swedenborg communicated, "but it is for the purpose of showing you the truths of your spirit-life, after the spirit has left the body, that we leave our high estate and the blissful life of the spheres, and come to teach you." [12]

Apparently, the spirits were experimenting on their side as well. The raps, taps, and tilting of tables turned into faster and more efficient forms of mediumship, including the automatic writing manifested by Dr. Dexter. Automatic writing has been perhaps the chief source of revelation. "Finally, after a long time, a message began to write itself on the paper," wrote the late Susy Smith in her 2000 book, *the Afterlife Codes*, of her introduction to automatic writing. "It was the most peculiar feeling I'd ever experienced. The hand was just writing by itself without my conscious will being involved in any way. It wrote scragglingly across the page in run-together words." [13]

Smith went on to become one of the best known modern day automatists, eventually moving from the pencil to the typewriter. "Can you imagine how it feels to sit at your typewriter and have your fingers type information that the mind does not consciously instigate, that you don't even know?" she added, going on to explain that her fingers seemed to move of their own volition and what they wrote was as different from what she wanted to say "as popcorn is from peanut butter." [14]

The initial messages purportedly came from her deceased mother, but her mother eventually introduced a new scribe, one who knew much more than she. He was identified as James Anderson, but Smith later discovered that Anderson was a pseudonym for William James, the famous philosopher and psychologist of a century ago. James explained that he used a pseudonym because he was concerned that Smith would have suspected he was a phony if he gave his true identity.

Another fairly recent automatic writer was Grace Rosher of England. In her 1961 book, *Beyond the Horizon*, Rosher explained that she was writing letters to friends one afternoon in 1957 when she heard, apparently clairaudiently, the words, "Leave your hands there and see what happens." To her amazement, the pen started to move without any effort on her part. Words began to form, and the message, "With love from Gordon," slowly appeared. Thus began her regular communication with Gordon Burdick, a long-deceased friend from her youth. Burdick described life on the Other Side and delivered many profound messages.

In the course of time, Rosher was told not to grasp the pen but to simply close her hand in a loose fist and to let the pen rest on top of it. The writing then flowed more fluently. "...I watched the pen move without any conscious effort on my part and write about things I had never dreamed of, and in a style of writing as different from my own as it could possibly be," Rosher explained. [15]

In the 1918 classic, *The Seven Purposes*, author Margaret Cameron described her sensation in automatic writing as "comparable to that of holding a quiet, live bird, wrapped in a handkerchief, its energy muffled but palpable. Sometimes this sensation of a current from without is communicated to the hand and arm, sometimes only to the fingers." [16]

Probably the most famous and studied case of automatic writing was that of Pearl Curran of St. Louis, Missouri. First from a friend's ouija board, then a pencil, then a typewriter, flowed the writings of a person identifying herself as Patience Worth, a 17th Century English woman. In some of her scripts, she used Anglo-Saxon words that are no longer part of the English vocabulary; yet, researchers were able to confirm that these words did exist at one time, although it was highly unlikely that Curran, a 31-year-old housewife with no more than an eighth-grade education, would have been exposed to them.

Over a period of 24 years, Patience Worth dictated approximately four million words, including seven books, some short stories, several plays, thousands of poems, and countless epigrams and aphorisms. She would be acclaimed a literary genius – her works compared with Shakespeare, Chaucer, and Spenser. She was called a wit, a poet, a dramatist, and a philosopher.

When a philologist asked Patience how and why she used the language of so many different periods, she responded: "I do plod a twist of a path and it hath run from then till now." When asked to explain how she could dictate responses without a pause, she replied: "Ye see, man setteth up his cup and fillet it, but I be as the stream." [17]

Among the many scholars and scientists who studied Pearl Curran was Dr. William E. Slaght, professor of psychology at Cornell University. "My tentative conclusion regarding this case is that we have here a manifestation of subconscious phenomena but in such unusual form that it differs entirely from the ordinary types," Slaght wrote. "In a few personalities, such as that of Mrs. Curran, it has been able to reach out beyond the ordinary boundaries of knowledge and come in touch with the springs of cosmic consciousness that gives deeper insight than any which comes through the ordinary channels of knowledge." [18]

While some automatic writing mediums go completely into a trance state, some into a semi-trance, others, like Pearl Curran, are fully awake and alert. In fact, Curran could carry on a conversation with others in the room while taking dictation from Patience Worth.

Like Slaght, a number of observers concluded that the wisdom was somehow coming from Pearl Curran's subconscious, but Dr. Walter Franklin Prince, who spent more time with Curran than anyone else, responded to this by saying that "either our concept of what we call the subconscious must be radically altered, so as to include potencies of which we hitherto have had no knowledge, or else some cause operating through but not originating in the subconsciousness of Mrs. Curran must be acknowledged." [19]

If the subconscious were playing tricks on them, both Smith and Rosher wondered how things they had never been exposed to or thought about got into the subconscious. Smith recognized that her own thoughts and beliefs were sometimes "coloring" the messages and worked diligently to "blank out" her mind.

Rosher consulted a graphologist who compared the handwriting with that in letters received from Burdick when he was alive and concluded that it was indeed the same. Rosher had never heard anything about Burdick's final days and asked him to provide her with some detail. He did, and she confirmed the information with mutual friends.

Burdick explained that in order to come into real and tangible contact with Rosher he had to get down to a lower vibration, something which he found very difficult at first but was able to perfect with practice.

William T. Stead*, a British journalist who went down with the Titanic, was an accomplished automatist. In one of his books, *Letters from Julia*, Stead wrote that he could not believe that any part of his unconscious self would deliberately practice a hoax upon his conscious self about the most serious of all subjects, and keep it up year after year with the most sincerity and consistency. "The simple explanation that my friend who has passed over can use my hand as her own seems much more natural and probable," concluded Stead, who was observed by Titanic survivors serenely sitting in the smoking room and reading his Bible as pandemonium took place all around him.[20]

With the possible exception of Pearl Curran, the most accomplished automatist of the 20th Century may have been Geraldine Cummins* of Ireland. In the Introduction of *The Road to Immortality*, published in 1932, Beatrice Gibbes described the method employed by Cummins. She would sit at a table, cover her eyes with her left hand and concentrate on "stillness." She would then fall into a light trance or dream state. Her hand would then begin to write. Usually, her spirit "control" would make some introductory remarks and announce that another entity was waiting to speak. Because of her semi-trance condition and also because of the speed at which the writing would come, Gibbes would sit beside her and remove each sheet of paper as it was filled. Cummins' hand was quickly lifted by Gibbes to the top of the new page, and the writing would continue without break. In one sitting, Gibbes stated, Cummins wrote 2,000 words in 75 minutes, whereas her normal compositions were laboriously put together, perhaps 800 words in seven or eight hours.

Gibbes added that she witnessed the writing of about 50 different personalities, all claiming to be "dead," all differing in character and style, coming through Cummins' hand.

The anonymous spirit communicating with John Scott of England, as documented in Scott's 1948 book, *As One Ghost to Another*, explained that "I send out my thought to your mind and it fuses with yours, and then you and I produce words together, which you, or rather we, write with your hand. There is no way of describing to you with your present knowledge the intricate process of communication." [21]

In the preface to the book, Scott states that he had previously regarded such things as "a pathetic delusion provoking humour in the daily press and anger in the churches." However, after he had retired to the country, he began experimenting with psychic matters and soon found that in his right hand a "vague urge." When he allowed his muscles to collaborate with the urge, he found his hand scrawling across the paper under it line after line in the semblance of writing. After some experimenting and practice the words became legible and made much sense.

At some point in the discourse, Scott asked his communicator why more spirits do not communicate in such a manner. "There are a few who at first return and communicate through your mediums, but their experience does not encourage them; in fact they soon despair of effecting any notable good," the communicating spirit told him, going on to inform him that it is very difficult to find minds which have the ability to receive such communication. "I think I may say that most of them become thus absorbed [with their new environment], to the exclusion of all thought of earth," the communicating spirit further told Scott, also mentioning that absolutely no communication comes through without a portion of error, which further frustrates communication.[22]

Scott concluded the preface of his book with the comment that the product of his hand has been laughed at by family and friends, while doctors have diagnosed him as suffering from a morbid state of schizophrenia. "I have broken into the shadowy abode of the suggested subconscious, seeking 'compensation for frustration' and 'escape,' thus letting loose an actor to simulate two dead persons, one not known to me at all and the other through hearsay," Scott wryly summarized one medical opinion.[23]

Another form of mediumship is referred to as the trance voice. Most notable among these mediums were Leonora Piper* of Boston, Massachusetts and Gladys Osborne Leonard* of England. Prominent author and publisher Dr. Henry Holt had several sittings with Piper. He related that after being seated a minute or two, her eyeballs rolled upward, her face became slightly convulsed, and then she began talking in a rough voice not her own. He recalled the voice affecting him as if it were coming from a statue, "pouring forth at one moment some brusquerie in the rough deep tones of Phinuit (her spirit control); at the next, in the same voice softened to gentleness, petting a child; then, perhaps, a return to the gruff tones in some biting sarcasm to some interloping control; then perhaps issuing from the same mouth, a child's voice singing the little boat song – all going on amid the weeping relatives who join in the song."[24]

Even more dynamic that the trance-voice phenomenon is the direct-voice, also called the independent voice. In this type of mediumship, the spirit voices come through several feet above the medium and are usually amplified by a "trumpet." Most mediums manifesting the direct voice do not go into a trance.

One of the best direct-voice mediums bringing through higher truths was Emily French*, of Rochester, New York. Edward C. Randall, a prominent Buffalo lawyer and corporate executive, had over 700 sittings with French, nearly all in his own home. "The room in which we hold communication with the spirits was constructed as directed by our spirit band," he explained. "It is consecrated to this work, and naught but harmony enters. In the day, the sun, so essential to life, floods it, and in the evening, when our labor begins, the curtains are drawn and darkness fills the room. Cloudlike substances form and change, evidence of gathering spirits. Magnetic and electric lights float and fall, but give forth no illumination. Then they greet us and we them, with words of welcome and fellowship, as do guests and host in any home. Usually, someone advanced in the other life is introduced, and he speaks on some special subject. In this manner, we are taught. We may ask for a lecture on any subject; and the same evening, or at a subsequent time, it will be given by a master mind. I have never heard such teachings and magnificent discourse in the material world. Our circle is known in that other life, and thousands are always waiting to come within the vibrations that have been formed."[25]

A much more rare form, even a century ago, was direct writing, in which the writing instrument would not require a hand to hold it. But the medium had to be nearby so that the communicating spirit could draw the necessary "energy" from him or her. Rosher's mediumship seems to have bordered on this, since she was able to simply have the pen rest on the top of her hand and not be grasped by her fingers.

Today, the "clairvoyant" or "clairaudient" type of mediumship, often witnessed on television with mediums like John Edward, James Van Praagh, and Lisa Williams, is more common. This type of mediumship usually involves brief evidential messages from deceased relatives or friends, often communicated symbolically. Such mediumship does not usually involve the communication of higher truths, wisdom, or philosophy that is the subject of this book. At the same time, the philosophical type of mediumship is usually not evidential, although evidential messages may sometimes come through the same medium, thereby giving added credibility to the philosophical messages. Of course, when the spirit's handwriting is the same or the voice is the same as when the spirit was incarnate, that is evidential to some extent.

People who have near-death experiences or who have learned to travel out of body, as well as those straddling the line between life and death, i.e., people on their deathbeds, may also have temporary clairvoyance and/or clairaudience, permitting them to pierce the veil. To the extent that they are able to report back on their experiences, they are also mediums. More of this type of mediumship is discussed in the next chapter.

Debunkers and skeptics seem to assume that communication between the spirit world and the material world should be as clear as if it were coming over the telephone. However, it is obvious from a number of messages that there are significant obstacles confronting the communicating spirits. To begin with, with the possible exception of the direct voice and direct writing, the messages must be filtered through the medium's mind. This results in unintentional distortion of the messages. Second, where a "spirit control" is involved, the control must interpret the thought images being given to him or her by the communicating spirit and may not interpret them correctly. When this spirit control passes on the messages, there may be further misinterpretation of the symbols or images being received by the medium. There are also indications that the communicating spirit is limited by the intelligence of the medium. Thus, if Einstein were trying to communicate a complex formula or a cure for cancer, he probably would not succeed unless the medium's intelligence is capable of grasping it. Moreover, one of the recurring messages of modern revelation is that we don't become all-knowing after death. For the most part, the spirits in the lower realms don't know much more now than they did when alive in the flesh.

Adding to the confusion, it appears that the more a spirit advances, the greater the difference in vibrational frequency between the spirit and the earth realm and the more difficult it is for that spirit to communicate with those of us on earth. In order to communicate, the advanced spirit must relay messages through spirits in lower realms. This can result in a distortion of messages as they are handed down to and through the earthly medium.

Soon after his death in 1892, George Pellew began communicating with Dr. Richard Hodgson through the trance mediumship of Leonora Piper. Hodgson, the chief investigator for the American Society for Psychical Research (ASPR), had been studying Mrs. Piper's mediumship for several years at that point. Pellew had been a member of the

ASPR before his death, resulting from a fall. As he communicated with Hodgson through Mrs. Piper, he told Hodgson of the difficulties he was encountering in communicating, pointing out that there is a conflict between the spiritual ego, or mind, of the communicating spirit and the material mind or ego of the medium that is very difficult to overcome. He explained that when Piper went into trance, her ego left the body, just as when a person is sleeping, and although her brain is left empty, it is very difficult for the communicating spirit to control it. He also mentioned that it was much easier to communicate with someone in "sympathy" with him, e.g., a friend or relative, than it was to communicate with a skeptical researcher. He said that to those in his sphere, we humans are "sleeping" in the material world and are what to them is a "dream-life." For them to communicate with us, they have to enter this sleep state, which adds to the confusion.

Apparently, few spirits are able to enter this "sleep state," and thus a spirit "control" is often necessary. This spirit control is able to enter the required state and relay messages on from those spirits who want to communicate but can't enter the state. Just as the medium on this side is acting as a "go-between," the spirit control functions as something of a "go-between" or medium on the other side of the veil. In the case of Mrs. Piper, a spirit named Phinuit, who claimed to have lived in France during the early part of the 19th Century, functioned as her control. Initially, he relayed messages from Pellew, but Pellew quickly learned how to enter the required state and was able to communicate directly. In fact, he took over as Mrs. Piper's primary control for a time.

All that is not to suggest that everything coming through mediums represents truth and revelation. Indeed, there are reasons for warnings in the Bible, as low-level and "earthbound" spirits are said to be closer to the earth vibration and therefore able to communicate more easily than more advanced spirits. These low-level spirits are apparently more interested in leading us astray than in providing us with wisdom or truth.

So, how can we know what to believe? As we are advised in 1 John 4:1, we must "test the spirits, as to whether they are of God," and we must "discern" the messages and constantly keep in mind Matthew 7:16, "By their fruits ye shall know them." If the messages can be reconciled with a just and loving Divinity and if they appeal to reason, they deserve some consideration. And when they come through again and again and again, as so many of the messages have, we should consider the possibility that there is something to them and that they are for our enlightenment and advancement.

Needless to say, mediumship is very complex and varies with the type of medium and the nature of her mediumship. Moreover, some mediums clearly are more developed than others. Which leads to the question why we don't have the quality of mediumship today that we had a century ago. There are a number of possible reasons for this, but the most prevalent one seems to be that people today don't have the quiet time they had before radio and television, and therefore they aren't aware of their ability or don't develop it. But another reason may very well be that the advanced spirits see no point in continuing to attempt to educate us, since we, especially orthodox religion, have obviously ignored their earlier teachings. After all, if some medium today were to report that she was receiving messages from Swedenborg, Bacon, Lincoln, or James, who would believe her? She would be diagnosed as delusional. What mainstream publisher would even consider offering the messages to the public? And what more might the advanced spirits say than has already been said through countless other mediums?

The skeptic naturally says that if there is a God, He should be able to communicate more effectively than He has or He should be able to facilitate communication by spirits. While communicating through a medium the renowned author and poet Victor Hugo once put this very question to a spirit claiming to be Martin Luther, the religious reformer, when alive, specifically asking why God doesn't better reveal Himself. The reply came, "Because doubt is the instrument which forges the human spirit. If the day were to come when the human spirit no longer doubted, the human soul would fly off and leave the plough behind, for it would have acquired wings. The earth would lie fallow. Now, God is the sower and man is the harvester. The celestial seed demands that the human ploughshare remain in the furrow of life." [26]

Factoring in John 16:12-14, as discussed in the Introduction, we are being given revelation as we can bear it, or understand it. If we were to be given absolute truth all at once, we would not be able to "bear it."

Communicating through William Stainton Moses* during the latter part of the 19th Century, the advanced spirit known as Imperator explained that the "Truth" will always be esoteric. "It must be so," Imperator stressed, "for only to the soul that is prepared can it be given. Its fragrance is too evanescent for daily common use. Its subtle perfume is shed only in the inner chamber of the spirit. Remember this; and remember too that violence is done to the Truth by forcing it on unprepared minds, while harm, great and far-reaching, is done to those who cannot receive what is a revelation to you but not to them."

Imperator added that the pursuit of Truth for its own sake is the highest aim of spirit on the earth plane of being, "higher than earth's ambitions, nobler than any work than man can do."[27]

[1] Hamilton, Trevor, *Immortal Longings*, imprint-academic.com, Exeter, UK, 2009, p. 80

[2] Myers, Frederic W. H., *Human Personality and Its Survival of Bodily Death*, University Books, Inc., New Hyde Park, NY, 1961

[3] Doyle, Arthur Conan, *The History of Spiritualism*, George H. Doran Co., New York, 1926, p. 57

[4] Edmonds, John W., and Dexter, George T., *Spiritualism*, Partridge & Brittan, New York, 1853, p. 81

[5] ___p. 84

[6] ___pp. 84-85

[7] ___pp. 85-86

[8] ___p. 88

[9] ___pp. 89-90

[10] ___pp. 91-92

[11] ___p. 93

[12] ___p.p. 96-97

[13] Smith, Suzy, *the Afterlife Codes*, Hampton Roads, Charlottesville, VA, 2000, p. 62

[14] ___p. 111

[15] Rosher, Grace, *Beyond the Horizon*, James Clarke & Co., London 1961, p. 9

[16] Cameron, Margaret, *The Seven Purposes*, Harper & Brothers, New York & London, 1918, p. 22

[17] Prince, Walter Franklin, *The Case of Patience Worth*, University Books, New Hyde Park, NY, 1964,

[18] ___pp. 69-70

[19] ___p. 509

[20] Stead, William T., *Letters from Julia*, The Progressive Thinker, Chicago, 1909, p. 6.

[21] Scott, John, *As One Ghost to Another*, Spiritualist Press Ltd., London, 1948, p. 12

[22] ___pp. 29-30

[23] ___p. 8

[24] Holt, Henry, *On the Cosmic Relations*, Houghton Mifflin Company, Boston and New York, 1914, p. 381

[25] Heagerty, N. Riley, *The French Revelation*, Morris Publishing, 2000, p. 31

[26] Chambers, John, *Conversations with Eternity: The Forgotten Masterpiece of Victor Hugo*, New Paradigm Books, Boca Raton, FL, 1998. p. 104

[27] Moses, William Stainton, *Spirit Teachings*, Arno Press, New York, 1976, pp. 283-284

2

APPROACHING DEATH

They come and they go and they trot and they dance, and never a word about death. All well and good. Yet, when death does come – to them, their wives, their children, their friends – catching them unawares and unprepared, then what storms of passion overwhelm them, what cries, what fury, what despair!

— Michel De Montaigne

The night before my 87-year-old mother died, she couldn't stop talking. While seemingly asleep, she jabbered away through the night. Because of her slurred speech resulting from several strokes, as well as advanced dementia, I couldn't make out what she was saying. However, she seemed to be desperately pleading with someone.

My wife and I had brought my mother up from her Berkeley, California rest home several days earlier to spend Thanksgiving 2003 with us at our Oregon home. We moved a spare bed into our bedroom so that we could better care for her. It was on the fourth or fifth night at our house, Thanksgiving night, that she began talking in her sleep.

The next morning, as I was carrying her from the bedroom downstairs to her wheelchair so that I could wheel her out to the car and drive her back to Berkeley, her eyes rolled back in her head and she "gave up the ghost."

In retrospect, I suspect that all the talking the prior night was with deceased loved ones who were trying to convince her that it was time to leave the physical world. Mom seemed very much afraid of dying when she was lucid. Whether that fear remained with her in her demented state, I have no idea, but I have no other explanation for her all-night chatter, other than the possibility that she was pleading with someone to help her disengage her spirit body from her weary physical shell.

More recently, my mother's sister passed on at age 81. My cousin informed me that her mother, my aunt, had many conversations with deceased loved-ones during the last week of her life.

Whether or not my mother and aunt actually communicated with deceased loves before they died, I have no way of knowing for sure, but I do know that there is considerable evidence to suggest that such deathbed visits are not unusual.

"They're so common I don't think much about them any more," said Ginny Chappelear, senior coordinator of bereavement services at the Tidewell Hospice in Sarasota, Florida, when I asked her if deathbed visions and visitations (DBVs) are common among hospice patients. "We call them the 'Gathering of Spirits'."

Chappelear, who has been doing hospice work for more than 20 years, recalled an early experience in which a woman was dying at home. "About five days before her death, she reported seeing a man looking in the window," Chappelear related. "This was out in the country and we were concerned that it was a peeping tom. But when the man came back she told us that it was her brother who had died many years earlier. 'He's just waiting for me,' she said. 'I'll go with him the next time he comes.' It was very comforting to her."

A more recent case involved a woman who was one of seven siblings and the sole survivor. "A day or two before she died, she started calling out the names of all her siblings," Chappelear remembered, "as if she were greeting them and saying 'Come on take me.'"

She recalled another case in which a father was dying and told his daughter that there was a loved one standing right there with her hands on his shoulders. "You can't see them," the dying man said, "but some day you'll understand what it is like."

For "people of faith" these visions and visitations make the dying process much easier, Chappelear added.

Skeptics say that the visions of the dying are nothing more than hallucinations. Of course they are if we define a hallucination as something outside of the range of the five ordinary senses. Such a definition does not mean it is not real, whatever "real" means.

Delusions perhaps? However, it is very difficult to discount certain cases. Consider that of "Jennie," and "Bessie" (both pseudonyms for privacy purposes) as related by Dr. Minot J. Savage, a popular Unitarian clergyman and author. Jennie and Bessie, ages 8-9, were close friends in a city in Massachusetts, and both were afflicted with diphtheria. Jennie died on Wednesday, but Bessie was not informed of her friend's death, as her family felt it might stand in the way of her recovery.

On Saturday, Bessie apparently realized that she was going to die and began telling her parents which of her brothers, sisters, and playmates should receive her treasured belongings. "Among these she pointed out certain things of which she was very fond, that were to go to Jennie – thus settling all question as to whether or not she had found out that Jennie was not still living," Savage wrote.

A little later, as she approached death, she began seeing deceased grandparents and others gathered around her bed. "And then she turned to her father, with face and voice both expressing the greatest surprise, and exclaimed, 'Why, Papa, why didn't you tell me that Jennie had gone? Why didn't you tell me of it?'" Savage ends the story, commenting that this and similar stories suggest that more than hallucination and imagination are involved.[1]

In his 1926 book, *Death-Bed Visions*, Sir William Barrett*, a professor of physics at the Royal College of Science in Dublin, reported on a case told to him by his wife, an obstetric surgeon. Lady (Florence) Barrett, who later became dean of the London School of Medicine for Women, was tending to a dying woman ("Mrs. B."), who had just given birth. Mrs. B. commented that it was getting "darker and darker." Her husband and mother were beckoned. "Suddenly she looked eagerly toward one part of the room, a radiant smile illuminating her whole countenance," Lady Barrett recalled. "Oh, lovely, lovely,' the dying woman said. Lady Barrett asked her to what she was referring. "What I see," the woman replied, "Lovely brightness, wonderful beings."[2]

The woman then began to focus her attention on one place in the room and cried out that her (deceased) father was there. Then, with a puzzled expression, she said that Vida, her sister, was with her father. Vida had died two weeks earlier, but because of Mrs. B's delicate condition, the family had decided not to tell her of her sister's death.

Scientist that he was, Sir William corroborated his wife's story by talking with a Dr. Phillips, another physician who had been present, as well as with the hospital matron, Miriam Castle.

In an earlier book, *On the Threshold of the Unseen*, Barrett printed a letter sent to him by a Dr. Wilson of New York, who was present at the last moments of James Moore, a well-known American tenor. Wilson told of being at Moore's bedside during the early morning. As he examined Moore, he noticed that his face was quite calm and his eyes clear. Moore then took the doctor's hand in both of his and thanked him for being such a good friend. "While he appeared perfectly rational and sane as any man I have ever seen," Wilson related, "the only way I can express it is that he was transported into another world, and although I cannot satisfactorily explain the matter to myself, I am fully convinced that he had entered the golden city – for he said in a stronger voice than he had used since I had attended him: 'There is mother! Why, mother, have you come to see me? No, no, I am coming to see you. Just wait, mother, I am almost over. Wait mother, wait, mother!'

"On his face there was a look of expressible happiness and the way in which he said the words impressed me as I have never been before, and I am as firmly convinced that he saw and talked with is mother as I am that I am sitting here." [3] Wilson went on to say that he immediately recorded every word and that it was the most beautiful death he had ever seen.

Barrett further reported on a case involving a young girl who was dying of consumption and had been seemingly unconscious and unaware of things going on around her when she opened her eyes and uttered the names of her three sisters, who had all died, as if recognizing their presence. Then, after a short pause, she said, "and Edward, too." [4] At the time, Edward, her brother, was thought to be alive in India, but word was later received that he had died in an accident a week or so prior to his sister's vision.

"The evidence seems indisputable that, in some rare cases, just before death the veil is partly drawn aside and glimpses of the loved ones who have passed over is given to the dying person," Barrett concluded. [5]

The Rev. Arthur Chambers, vicar of the Church of England in Brockenhurst, Hampshire, England, reported that a dying man said to him, "You consider, do you not, that my mind is perfectly clear?" Chambers assured him that he did and that he had never known him to be more so. "Very well, then," the dying man continued. "Now I want to tell you what occurred last evening. But first you must understand that I was neither dreaming nor under a delusion. As I lay here, my father, who died some years ago, stood in the place where you are now and spoke to me. He told me I had only a very little longer to remain on earth, and said that he and other dear ones passed away were waiting to welcome me into the spiritual world. I tried to raise myself in bed, in order to attract the attention of the nurse who was at the other end of the ward. I thought you might still be in the building, and I wanted her to send for you, that you, too, might see my father. I supposed the effort to raise myself must have been too much for me, for I slipped back on the pillow and felt I was fainting. When I opened my eyes again, I looked for my father, but he was gone. Don't tell me I was dreaming, because I tell you with my dying breath I was not. My father was as real there as you are now, and I think he will come again." [6]

The man died two days later, after which Chambers spoke to a man in a nearby bed. Without knowing what the dying man had told Chambers, the patient informed Chambers that just before the man died he saw him raise himself into a sitting position, fix his gaze earnestly on the spot where Chambers had so often prayed and conversed with him, smile, as if he were recognizing someone, and then fall back on his pillow motionless. A minute or two later, the screen was put around the bed, and he knew the man was gone.

Dr. Reginald Hegy, an Irish physician, told of attending a patient who had suddenly taken ill but did not appear terminal. However, the patient insisted she was about to die. "After the farewells had been made, sitting bolt upright in bed and turning to the side of the bed at which there was apparently nobody, her facial expression suddenly changed from one of intense suffering to one of extreme happiness and pleasure as if an unexpected but most welcome visitor had just appeared," Hegy wrote. "Then she fell back – dead. The whole event lasted but an instant, but the surprise and joy of the patient were so vivid that I myself could not help looking to see who had arrived. I saw no one of course. The incident impressed me deeply, as it would anyone who had witnessed it, for everything seemed to indicate that some person invisible to us, but clearly visible to the dying woman, had appeared. Her premonition of impending death is also significant. This experience is by no means an isolated one." [7]

Hegy reported another deathbed scene which left a lasting impression on him. It involved an elderly woman, who had been comatose and was expected to die at any time. "Most unexpectedly a period of consciousness ensued when those around the bedside were surprised to hear the patient calmly state that she had just seen her husband who had died thirty years previously, and had been told that her time to pass over had not yet come and that she would remain on earth three days longer," Hegy recorded. "She also gave a message to her nurse (a widow), which she said was from this lady's deceased husband. The message proved to be remarkably relevant. After this period of lucidity the state of unconsciousness again supervened, and lasted three days, at the end of which time death took place as the patient had herself foretold." [8]

In her book, *They Walked Among Us*, Louie Harris recalled the passing of her father. He whispered to his wife that it was time for him to leave and apologized for not being able to bid farewell to Ted, their son, who was serving in the British army in France. "Father was quiet for some time," Harris wrote. "His eyes were closed. Then, quite unexpectedly, he sat up unaided, his eyes open, his face radiant. He stretched out his arms and joyfully exclaimed: 'George! Austin!' These were the names of his 'dead' brothers. A beautiful smile transformed his thin face. With a deep sigh of satisfaction he lay back on his pillow and passed peacefully to the spirit world." [9]

More recently, the subject of deathbed visions and visitations was discussed by Dr. Elisabeth Kübler-Ross, the physician who revolutionized our approach to dying and death. She pointed out that many dying children become aware that they have the ability to leave the physical body and experience the presence of those who surround them, guide them, and help them. "Young children often refer to them as their playmates," she wrote. "The churches have called them guardian angels. Most researchers would call them guides." [10]

Kübler-Ross mentioned a typical case (for her) in which a mother, son, and daughter all perished in an automobile accident. While the mother expired at the scene of the accident, the two children survived long enough to be taken to separate hospitals. As Kübler-Ross sat with the dying girl, the child mentioned that her mother and her brother were waiting for her. It was not until later that Kübler-Ross found out that the boy had died before the girl made her statement about him.

E. Beatrice Gibbes, a researcher who dedicated much of her life to observing and assisting Geraldine Cummins*, the renowned Irish automatic writing medium, reported on a case involving Mrs. Napier Webb, an old friend of Miss Cummins', in a 1945 issue of *Light* magazine. Mrs. Webb was seriously injured in a hunting accident during March 1944. Brain surgery was performed during May and it was considered doubtful that she would survive it. On the evening of May 25, Gibbes and Cummins were supposed to go to tea and then a film in London, but Cummins had a sudden urge to write. After Cummins was seated and went into a trance with pen in hand, Astor, her spirit control, communicated that a strange woman was close by but he didn't know what she wanted. Before Gibbes, who was seated at the table, could finish telling Astor to ask her who she was and what she wanted, the pen appeared to be seized and wrote "Tid Webb." Tid was the pet name of Mrs. Webb. She wrote: "My dear Geraldine. It is strange how my thoughts have gone out to you in this dreadful time. I am in two worlds. I am not dead but I may be soon. I can't talk to anyone. I want to tell them things: how I was with B___ (her son killed in Hong Kong early in the war). He took me into a world so brilliant I can't describe it. This is just a little visit to beg you, if you go over to Ireland, not to lose sight of my darling...(her young and only daughter). The boys are all right but she is so young...The doctor has been here and I could see that he still thinks I have a little chance – that I may struggle back, and I want to so much, perhaps I shall. If I don't recover, promise me you will do as I ask." [11]

Gibbes replied to Mrs. Webb, explaining that Cummins was in a trance but that she would inform her of the request as soon as she was fully conscious. Webb replied: "Oh, Miss Gibbes. Of course I see you now. Thank you so much. Now that queer cord is beginning to pull at me." Gibbes asked her if she was in a coma at the time. "I saw my body lying there and I am still bound to it by a silvery cord – a bit frayed, you know," Webb responded. [12]

Astor took back control and told Gibbes that he did not think that the woman had passed over because he could see the cord of life still there. But he could tell that she was in and out of her body. A mutual friend later wrote to Cummins and said that Mrs. Webb was still alive but that she appeared to be "half or more than half with the others, and only comes back with an effort when one comes in and speaks." [13] She died about three months after the sitting.

Similarly, trance medium and clairvoyant Gladys Osborne Leonard* reported seeing and communicating with her husband's spirit body before he actually died. With a nurse watching over her husband, who had been very ill for a number of days but seemed to be improving, Mrs. Leonard took a walk on the beach outside of their cottage. She became aware of a vague, shadowy form walking next to her and talking to her. "Don't worry, little woman, don't worry," her husband told her. Thinking he might have died, Leonard raced home and found her husband in a deep sleep. When he awoke he told her that he had been out on the seafront and was talking to people, although he did not remember talking to Gladys. "This experience made me quite certain that my husband's soul body was loosening its hold on the physical counterpart in spite of the recent improvement in his condition," Leonard wrote, further mentioning that she had clairvoyantly witnessed the "double" of several other people before their actual deaths.[14]

At the bicentenary celebration of the Royal Medical Society in 1937, Sir Auckland Geddes, a British surgeon turned statesman, reported on the strange experience of a man who did not want to be identified but whose credibility Geddes said he could not question. Indications were, however, that it was Geddes' own experience.

The experiencer reported that on November 9, 1935, a few minutes after midnight, he began to feel very ill. By 2 a.m., he realized he was suffering from acute gastro-enteritis, which kept him vomiting and purging until about 8 a.m. By 10 a.m., he concluded that he had developed all the symptoms of a very acute poisoning, including intense gastro-intestinal pain, diarrhea, and with "pulse and respiration quite impossible to count." He wanted to ring for assistance, but could not. Realizing that he was very ill, he quickly reviewed his financial position.

"...at no time did my consciousness appear to me to be in any way dimmed, but I suddenly realized that *my* consciousness was separating from another consciousness, which was also me," the experiencer reported. "These for purposes of description we could call the A and B consciousness, and throughout what follows, the ego attached itself to the A consciousness."

The experiencer recognized that the B personality belonged to the body. As his condition grew worse, he noticed that his heart was fibrillating rather than beating. "I realized that the B consciousness belonging to the body was beginning to show signs of becoming composite, that is, built up of 'consciousness' from the head, the heart and the viscera. These components became more individual, and the B consciousness began to disintegrate, while the A consciousness which was now me, seemed to be altogether outside my body, which it could see. Gradually I realized that I could see not only my body and the bed in which it was, but everything in the whole house and garden, and then I realized that I was seeing not only 'things' at home, but in London and Scotland, in fact wherever my attention was directed it seemed to me; and the explanation which I received, from what source I do not know, but which

I found myself calling to myself my mentor, was that I was free in a time dimension of space, wherein 'now' was in some way equivalent to 'here' in the ordinary three-dimension space of everyday life."

The experiencer then realized that his vision included not only "things" in the ordinary three-dimensional world, but also "things" in the four or more dimensional places in which he found himself.

"From now on the description is and must be entirely metaphorical," he continued, "because there are no words which really describe what I saw, or rather appreciated. Although I had no body, I had what appeared to be perfect two-eyed vision, and what I saw can only be described in this way, that I was conscious of a psychic stream flowing with life through time, and this gave me the impression of being visible, and it seemed to me to have particularly intense iridescence. I understood from my mentor that all our brains are just end organs projecting as it were from the three-dimensional universe into the psychic stream, and flowing with it into the fourth and fifth dimensions."

Around each brain, as the experiencer saw it, there seemed to be a condensation of the psychic stream, which appeared as a small cloud. "While I was just appreciating this, the mentor who was conveying information to me explained that the fourth dimension was in everything existing in the three-dimensional space, and at the same time everything in the three-dimensional space existed in the fourth dimension, and also in the fifth dimension, and I at the time quite clearly understood what was meant, and quite understood how 'now' in the fourth-dimensional universe was just the same to all intents and purposes as 'here' in a three-dimensional view of things...I then realized that I myself was a condensation, as it were, in the psychic stream, a sort of cloud that was not a cloud, and the visual impression I had of myself was blue."

Gradually, the experiencer began to recognize a number of people he knew and saw the "psychic condensation" attached to them. He also saw a number of people who had very little psychic condensation attached to them. He saw different colors – blue, purple and dark red, pink, grey-brown, pearly, apricot, and brown around various acquaintances. As he was observing all of this, he saw the woman with the purple and dark red condensation enter the room and hurry to the telephone to call his doctor.

Upon his initial examination, the treating physician commented, "He is nearly gone." The experiencer heard him clearly speaking to him on the bed, but could not reply. "I was really cross when he took a syringe and rapidly injected my body with something which I afterwards learned was camphor," the experiencer continued his account. "As the heart began to beat more strongly, I was drawn back, and I was intensely annoyed, because I was so interested, and just beginning to understand where I was and what I was 'seeing.' I came back into the body really angry at being pulled back, and once I was back all the clarity of vision of anything and everything disappeared, and I was just possessed of a glimmer of consciousness which was suffused with pain."

The experiencer went on to say that the "dream, vision, or experience has shown no tendency to fade like a dream would fade, nor has it shown any tendency that I am aware of to grow or to rationalize itself as a dream would do." Further, he had had no repetition of any sort or kind of the experience of clear understanding that he had experienced while "free from the body." [15]

As Fanny Ruthven Paget, a resident of Houston, Texas, suffered from pneumonia and straddled the line between life and death during 1911, she found herself looking down at her body resting peacefully on the bed. After studying her body in detail, she began to concern herself with her fiancé in another town. She then found herself being propelled by a vibratory sensation to his sleeping body. "As I looked upon him I saw the shadow body more distinctly than the physical," she wrote. "Viewed from the other side of life, the 'shadow' body seemed the original and the physical the duplicate, the soul the real, the body the unreal. Within and interpenetrating all was a light, which I had not before perceived as being a part of the spiritual anatomy. This light penetrated from within, both the shadow and physical bodies, maintaining through and about the body an aura or illumination which enveloped it; clothing it, as it were, in a magnetized illumination. How wonderful this three-in-one life-manifestation seemed, especially when we generally recognize only the one – the physical!"

Moving closer to her fiancé, Paget attempted to converse with him, but he slept on, even though his soul, which was not sleeping, responded joyously and tried to help her penetrate his physical consciousness as he moaned and turned restlessly in his sleep. After a few moments, he cried out, "Fanny, Fanny," and sat up in bed, wide awake. As he turned on a light and reached for his glasses and a magazine, she tried to communicate, but he did not react to her words. "I am dead, that is why he cannot hear and see me," she thought, further recalling that she felt more alive than she had ever felt. "There was something pitiably painful about being so near one beloved, seeing him plainly and hearing him distinctly, even knowing that he was thinking of me, and yet having him utterly ignore my presence, and above all knowing that he would never recognize me again – never hear my voice no matter how ardently I called, while I was the same in every way minus the physical body."

Then she perceived that her vibratory environment did not harmonize with his. "Mine was the vibration of perpetual motion – his more like a 'dead sea' into which these vibratory currents ebbed and flowed, and it seemed such an easy matter to move out of the 'deadness' into the 'ebb and flow' that I waited and watched a long time before I realized that he would make no effort to do so."

Realizing that she would not be able to penetrate his physical consciousness, she bade him farewell and attempted to move on; however, the vibratory force seemed to restrain her. "Persistently the force held me, as though inviting me to further considerations of earth interests, but I had none. My material possessions were disposed of as I desired; there was no life-work I was leaving incomplete; I had no children, no one depending on me; nothing held me to the earth. My desire had been to go beyond it and now that I had done so, I was well pleased and wanted to go on to the joys I felt awaited me beyond the influence of earth. Yet the force held me, try as I would to pass beyond it, until, instead of struggling against it I tried to understand it – to wrest from it its reason for thus detaining me, feeling that there must be some reason for such marked persistence. Almost instantly the lesson sank into my consciousness and I realized that the long arm of mundane interests can reach into the Beyond and hold its victims within the shadow of earth – pitting its magnetism against the promise of higher things."[16]

Much more recently, the subject has been explored by Carla Wills-Brandon, Ph.D. in her book, *One Last Hug Before I Go*, and by Dr. Peter Fenwick, an internationally renowned British neuro-psychiatrist, and Elizabeth Fenwick in their 2008 book, *The Art of Dying*.

Wills-Brandon looks at the various theories advanced by materialistic scientists to explain away such visions, including mental illness, excessive grief, wishful thinking, hysteria, drug-induced hallucinations of an overactive imagination, and the by-product of random firings of a dying brain, concluding that many deathbed visions, especially those involving visions of deceased loved ones whose death was unknown to the dying person, go beyond any of these theories. She laments the fact that such explanations take away from the spiritual significance of such encounters and that caregivers frequently ignore them.

The Fenwicks found that drug- and fever-induced hallucinations are quite different from true end-of-life visions and that they have quite a different effect on patients. Drug or fever-induced hallucinations, including such things as seeing animals walking around on the floor, children running in and out of the room, devils or dragons dancing in the light, or insects moving in wall-paper or on the carpet, are rarely, if ever, comforting. "True deathbed hallucinations are quite different," they state. "They are not confusional. Most occur in full consciousness; often, moreover, an unconscious patient will regain consciousness and see the vision in a brief lucid interval before they die." [17]

Like Wills-Brandon, the Fenwicks lament the fact that many caregivers are not trained or prepared to deal with this aspect of the dying process. In fact, many of them do not discuss it as they fear ridicule.

In what has been in all likelihood the most extensive study of deathbed visions, Karlis Osis, Ph.D. and Erlendur Haraldsson, Ph.D. interviewed more than 1,000 doctors and nurses who had responded to a questionnaire asking about deathbed observations. In order to avoid a religious bias, the researchers carried out the study in both the United States and India. Operating under the auspices of The American Society for Psychical Research, Osis and Haraldsson reported their findings in a 1977 book, *At the Hour of Death.*

According to the two researchers, the study had built-in checks and balances on possible sources of respondent biases, such as religious beliefs, attitudes toward hallucinations, length of contact with the patient, patient load, and relationship to the patient, i.e., friend or relative. They found underreporting by young doctors, especially in the U.S, leading them to conclude that their study showed a lesser proportion of afterlife-related experiences than there actually were. Moreover, patients seemed to be hesitant to reveal their otherworldly experiences to skeptical physicians and nurses.

Osis and Haraldsson found a significant number of cases where patients died in accordance with the "call" of an apparition, even when the medical prognosis was for recovery. These apparitions, they noted, seemed to show a will of their own, instead of expressing the desires and inner dynamics of the patients. Nearly all the American patients, and two-thirds of the Indian patients, were ready to go after having seen otherworldly apparitions with a take-away purpose. Encounters with the apparitions seemed to be so gratifying that the value of this life was easily outweighed.

"The same patients who were in pain, who were miserable and scared, seemed to take a peek at the 'other world' reality and become 'exultant' and 'radiant' – eager to go into it," they explained, pointing out that it does not seem to matter even to young people.[18] Such was the case reported by Dr. W. T. O'Hara, medical officer on a White Star ship. An orphan girl of 10 was on the ship in the charge of the captain during a voyage in the China Sea. She fell ill and it was clear to O'Hara that death was near. As he sat next to her, O'Hara sensed a presence in the room but was unable to see it. As he checked the girl's pulse and determined that her heart was still beating, the room grew brighter and seemed to gather in waves of blue and white and gold over the child's body. The girl looked up and murmured, "Oh, look! How beautiful!" at which time O'Hara saw a misty, luminous globe over her head. The girl then cried out, "Oh Mamma...I see...the way...and it is all bright and shining."[19] Then the light rose rapidly and disappeared at the ceiling, at which time the girl died. When the captain entered the cabin, he told O'Hara that he and four other officers, who came with him, had seen a ball of blue fire right over their heads in the smoking room. They observed it float to the door and turn toward the cabin occupied by O'Hara and the young girl.

Osis and Haraldsson also found that there were some rare cases in which the patients, although incoherent or suffering from brain disease or schizophrenia, became lucid and their normal selves shortly before death. Moreover, serenity, peace, and religious emotion did not correlate with moods of the day before. Thus, a patient might have been in complete despair before experiencing the vision or apparition.

The two researchers further noted that only a small minority of the patients who had deathbed visions had received drugs. Those who had received medication had no greater frequency of afterlife visions than the other patients.

"This finding is loud and clear," Osis and Haraldsson stressed. "When the dying see apparitions, they are nearly always experienced as messengers from a postmortem mode of existence. Of the human figures seen in visions of the dying, the vast majority were deceased close relatives."[20] They added that hallucinations of mental patients and drug-induced visions seldom portrayed close relatives.

Osis and Haraldsson also observed that some dying patients seemed to be free of pain and discomfort at those moments when they appeared to see through the veil. As reported in the *Journal* of the American Society for Psychical Research for June 1918, Daisy Dryden, age 10, of

California, was suffering from typhoid fever and began suffering greatly four days before her death as enteritis set in. After about 24 hours of excruciating pain, Daisy seemed to become clairvoyant and the pain passed. During her final three days she reported talking with her deceased brother, Allie, who had died of scarlet fever seven months earlier. When her Sunday school teacher, "Mrs. H.", was sitting with her two days before her death, Daisy told her that her two children were there. Mrs. H. was stymied, as she was certain that Daisy could not have known about her two children who had died some years before, and asked Daisy to describe them. When Daisy described them as adults, Mrs. H. informed her children were not adults when they died. Daisy replied: "Allie says, 'Children do not stay children; they grow up as they do in this life."

When Lulu, Daisy's sister, spoke to Daisy of angels with "snowy wings," Daisy told her that the ones she had seen didn't have wings. When Lulu asked how they could fly down from heaven without wings, Daisy replied that "they just come." When Daisy was asked how she speaks to Allie, she responded that "We just talk with our think."

When Daisy's mother was sitting at her bedside, Daisy mentioned that Allie was standing next to her. When the mother looked for Allie, Daisy told her that Allie said she could not see him because her spirit eyes were closed, but that she (Daisy) could see him because her body only holds her spirit by a thread of life.

At 8:30 on the evening of her death, Daisy informed her mother that Allie would be coming for her at 11:30. At 11:15, Daisy asked her father to take her up as Allie had come. As they sang, Daisy breathed her last at 11:30. [21]

In his 2010 book *Glimpses of Eternity*, Dr. Raymond Moody, who is known primarily for his pioneering work in near-death experiences, tells of being at the bed of his dying mother with other family members in 1994. As they gathered around their mother's bed waiting for the moment of death, Moody's sister claimed to see their deceased father. The others didn't see him, but they all reported seeing an unusual light in the room. "It was like looking at light in a swimming pool at night," Moody wrote, adding that "it was as though the fabric of the universe had torn and for just a moment we felt the energy of that place called heaven." [22]

There are countless such reports of dying people having visions of light and seeing loved ones gathering, but skeptics discount them, calling them hallucinations. However, as Moody points out, it is one thing to claim that the dying person is hallucinating, quite another to claim that healthy people in the room are sharing in the hallucination with the dying person.

All of the aforementioned cases involve people on their deathbeds. What about those who meet death accidentally? American doctors William Green, Stefan Goldstein and Alex Moss reportedly researched thousands of stories about patients who died suddenly and unexpectedly. They concluded that most people had anticipated their own death. While the majority of them may not have understood their premonitions, there was something at the deep soul level or in the subconscious that at least alerted them to the fact that death was approaching.

Thus, it would seem that whether the person is on his or her deathbed or about to die unexpectedly, the soul knows beforehand that transition is about to take place. It may be that the more conscious, i.e., spiritually awakened, the person, the closer the awareness is to the conscious self.

(The subject of precognition or premonitions of death is discussed further in Appendix A)

[1] Savage, Minot J., *Life Beyond Death*, G.P. Putnam's Sons, New York, NY, 1900, pp. 310-311

[2] Barrett, Sir William, *Death-Bed Visions*, The Aquarian Press, Northhamptonshire, England, 1986, p. 11

[3] Barrett, Sir William, *On the Threshold of the Unseen*, E. P. Dutton & Co. New York, NY, 1918, pp. 158-159

[4] _____ p. 159

[5] _____ p. 160

[6] Chambers, Arthur, *Man and the Spiritual World*, George W. Jacobs & Co., Philadelphia, 1900, pp. 108-109

[7] Hegy, Reginald, *A Witness Through the Centuries*, E. P. Dutton & Co., Inc. New York, NY, 1935, pp. 24-25

[8] _____ pp. 25-26

[9] Harris, Louie, *They Walked Among Us*, Pyschic Press Ltd., London, 1980, p. 13

[10] Kubler-Ross, Elisabeth, *On Life After Death*, Celestial Arts, Berkeley, Calif., p. 51

[11] Cummins, Geraldine, *Mind in Life and Death*, The Aquarian Press, London, 1956, p. 91

[12] _____ p. 91

[13] _____ p. 92.

[14] Leonard, Gladys Osborne, *The Last Crossing*, Psychic Book Club, London, 1937, pp. 28-29

[15] _____ pp. 96-97

[16] Paget, Fanny Ruthven, *How I Know That the Dear are Alive*, Plenty Publishing Co., Washington, D.C., 1917, pp. 160-166

[17] Fenwick, Peter & Elizabeth, *The Art of Dying*, Continuum, New York, NY, 2008, p. 83

[18] Osis, Karlis and Haraldsson, Erlendur, *At the Hour of Death*, Avon Books, New York, 1977, pp. 34-35.

[19] Cooke, Aileen H., *Out of the Mouth of Babes*, James Clarke & Co., Ltd., London, 1968, pp. 71-72

[20] Osis, pp. 184-185.

[21] De Brath, Stanley, *Psychical Research Science and Religion*, Methuen & Co., London, 1925, pp. 136-141

[22] Moody, Raymond, *Glimpses of Eternity*, Guideposts, New York, NY, 2010, pp. 49-50..

3

GIVING UP THE GHOST

Or ever the silver cord be loosed, or the golden bowl be broken, or the pitcher be broken at the fountain, or the wheel broken at the cistern. Then shall the dust return to the earth as it was: and the spirit shall return unto God who gave it.
— **Ecclesiastes 12:6-7**

One Bible reference suggests that the Old Testament passage quoted above should be interpreted by taking the "silver cord" to mean the marrow of the backbone, the "golden bowl" to mean the membrane that covers the brain, the "pitcher" to mean the veins of the body, the "fountain" to mean the liver, the "wheel" to mean the head, and the "cistern" to mean the heart out of which the head draws the power of life.

Ecclesiastes seems to suggest that the loosening of the "silver cord" is one of several ways by which the physical body and spirit body separate at the time of death, perhaps referring to old age. Clairvoyants, out-of-body travelers, and spirit communicators, however, see the severance of the silver cord involved in every kind of death. This cord is said to be the counterpart of the umbilical cord of birth. While the umbilical cord must be severed when we come into the material world, the silver cord must be severed when we return to the *real* world. This severance is sometimes referred to as "giving up the ghost" or, as Shakespeare called it, "shuffling off this mortal coil."

Frederic W. H. Myers*, the Cambridge scholar who became a pioneering psychical researcher, communicated extensively through the mediumship of Geraldine Cummins* of Ireland, perhaps the most famous and credible automatic writing medium ever, after his death in 1901. Myers referred to the spirit body as the "double," explaining that it is an exact counterpart of the physical shape. "The two are bound together by many little threads, by two silver cords," Myers communicated. "One of these makes contact with the solar plexus, the other with the brain. They all may lengthen or extend during sleep or during half-sleep, for they have considerable elasticity. When a man slowly dies these threads and two cords are gradually broken. Death occurs when these two principal communicating lines with brain and solar plexus are severed." [1]

Myers went on to explain that life occasionally lingers in certain cells of the body after the soul has departed and that during this time the double is still attached to the physical shell by some threads which have not been broken. However, he pointed out that the soul does not suffer during this time. As a rule, Myers stated, the soul achieves complete freedom within an hour or two or three of physical death. He added that there is usually no pain connected with the separation.

According to Myers, death results from a change in vibration, the physical body vibrating at a much slower rate than the "double." There is a temporary dislocation as the soul passes from the confines of the physical body to the spirit body.

While Myers and others have referred to the spirit body as the double, it has been given different names, including etheric body, astral body, subtle body, celestial body, soul body, ghost, odic body, radiant body, perispirit, and phantom, to name just some. However, there are indications that there are two or three bodies besides the physical body. In Theosophy, the etheric body, or double, is a subtle interpenetrating extension of the physical body. It is this body that is held to the physical body by the silver cord. At some point, the astral body separates from the etheric body.

Estelle Roberts, one of England's most famous mediums, recalled being at the bedside of her husband, Hugh, as he died. Her clairvoyance allowed her to see his spirit leave his body from his head and mold itself into an exact replica of his physical body. She observed a cord connecting the two bodies. When the cord broke, the spirit body floated away and passed through the wall. She also reported hearing strange, terrifying noises as if someone was "rending linen" and occasionally sounding like the cracking of a whip. This apparently was the spirit body breaking loose from the physical body.[2]

Long before Dr. Raymond Moody published his findings on near-death experiences, Dr. A. S. Wiltse, a Kansas physician, reported a personal experience which was no doubt a near-death experience, as he suffered from typhoid fever. He was informed by his attending physician, Dr. S. H. Raynes, that he was without pulse or perceptible heartbeat for about four hours. "Dr. Raynes informs me, however, that by bringing his eyes close to my face, he could perceive an occasional short gasp, so very light as to be barely perceptible, and that he was upon the point, several times of saying, 'He is dead,' when a gasp would occur in time to check him."

During the time that he appeared to be dead, Wiltse curiously observed what was going on. "With all the interest of a physician, I beheld the wonders of my bodily anatomy, intimately interwoven with which, even tissue for tissue, was I, the living soul of that dead body. I learned that the epidermis was the outside boundary of the ultimate tissues, so to speak, of the soul. I realized my condition and reasoned calmly thus. I have died, as men term death, and yet I am as much a man as ever. I am about to get out of the body. I watched the interesting process of the separation of soul and body. By some power, apparently not my own, the Ego was rocked to and fro, laterally, as a cradle is rocked, by which process its connection with the tissues of the body was broken up. After a little time the lateral motion ceased, and long the soles of the feet beginning at the toes, passing rapidly to the heels, I felt and heard, as it seemed, the snapping of innumerable small cords. When this was accomplished, I began slowly to retreat from the feet, toward the head, as a rubber cord shortens. I remember reaching the hips and saying to myself, 'Now, there is no life below the hips.'"

Dr. Wiltse could not recall passing through the abdomen or chest, but he recollected that his "whole self" was collected into his head. He appeared to himself something like a jelly-fish in color and form and remembered thinking that he would soon be free.

"As I emerged from the head, I floated up and down and laterally like a soap bubble attached to the bowl of a pipe until I at last broke loose from the body and fell lightly to the floor, where I slowly arose and expanded into the full stature of a man. I seemed to be translucent, of a bluish cast and perfectly naked. With a painful sense of embarrassment,

I fled toward the partially opened door to escape the eyes of the two ladies whom I was facing, as well as others who I knew were about me, but upon reaching the door I found myself clothed, and satisfied upon that point, I turned and faced the company."

To Wiltse's surprise, the arm of one man standing near the door passed through his arm without resistance. The man gave no sign of the contact or of seeing Wiltse as he continued to gaze toward the couch. "I directed my gaze in the direction of his and saw my own dead body."

Wiltse recalled being surprised at how pale the body looked but congratulated himself on the way he had composed his body, his hands clasped at his chest. He marveled at how well he was feeling, when only minutes before he was in extreme distress. He then looked back through the open door, where he could see his body. "I discovered then a small cord, like a spider's web, running from my shoulders (of the spirit body) back to my body and attaching to it at the base of my neck in front."

He then attempted to gain the attention of the people gathered in the room, but he was unsuccessful. "It did not once occur to me to speak, and I concluded the matter by saying to myself; 'They see only with the eyes of the body. They cannot see spirits. They are watching what they think is I, but they are mistaken. That is not I. This is I and I am as much alive as ever.'"

Since no one was giving any attention to the real "him," Wiltse wandered outside. "I never saw the street more distinctly than I saw it then," he continued. "I took note of the redness of the soil and of the washes the rain had made. I took a rather pathetic look about me, like one who is about to leave his home for a long time. Then I discovered that I had become larger than I was in earth life and congratulated myself thereupon. I was somewhat smaller in the body than I just liked to be, but in the next life, I thought, I am to be as I desired."

He soon became aware of a "presence," which he could not see, but which he knew was entering into an overhead cloud from the southern side. "The presence did not seem, to my mind, as a form, because it filled the cloud like some vast intelligence... Then from the right side and from the left of the cloud a tongue of black vapor shot forth and rested lightly upon either side of my head, and as they touched me thoughts not my own entered into my brain. "These, I said, are his thoughts and not mine; they might be in Greek or Hebrew for all power I have over them. But how kindly am I addressed in my mother tongue that so I may understand all his will. Yet, although the language was English, it was so eminently above my power to reproduce that my rendition of it is far short of the original. The following is as near as I can render it:

'This is the road to the eternal world. Yonder rocks are the boundary between the two worlds and the two lives. Once you pass them, you can no more return into the body. If your work is complete on earth, you may pass beyond the rocks. If, however, upon consideration you conclude that...it is not done, you can return into the body.'"

Wiltse approached the rocks. "I was tempted to cross the boundary line. I hesitated and reasoned thus: 'I have died once and if I go back, soon or late, I must die again. If I stay someone else will do my work, and so the end will be as well and as surely accomplished, and shall I die again? I will not, but now that I am so near I will cross the line and stay."

But as he attempted to cross the line, a black cloud appeared in front of him. "I knew that I was to be stopped. I felt the power to move or to think leaving me. My hands fell powerless at my side, my head dropped forward, the cloud touched my face and I knew no more." In "astonishment and disappointment," Wiltse then found himself back in his physical body. "What in the world has happened to me? he exclaimed. "Must I die again?"[3]

Since Wiltse returned to life, the cord apparently was not severed.

Much more recently, in their 2008 book, *The Art of Dying*, Dr. Peter Fenwick of England and his wife, Elizabeth Fenwick, quote one NDEr as feeling "like a kite on an endless string." This "cord" seemed to be attached to the back and the person could feel it pulling her back into her body. Another NDEr told the Fenwicks that although he could not see his body, he could see that he was attached by a "light grey rope."

Dr. Sam Parnia, another NDE researcher, was told by an experiencer that she found herself standing beside herself looking at a cord that connected her to her body and thinking how thin and wispy it was.

Communicating through the direct-voice mediumship of Lilian Bailey, Bill Wootton, a World War I victim, described the life cord as silver and thick, glowing and glistening. He said that it emerges from the pineal gland in the head and extends to the solar plexus. Wooten added that spirits are able to tell the health of a person by the cord. When they see the cord getting down to a hair's breadth, they know that the cord is about to snap. When it does snap, it is as if a rope were breaking, and death then takes place.[4]

Wellesley Tudor Pole, a British medium and mystic, reported on his experiences as he sat with a dying friend, whom he refers to as "Major

P." Death seemed close at hand as Major P. remained unconscious. Pole noticed a shadowy form hovering in a horizontal position about two feet above the bed. "This form is attached to the physical body on the bed by two transparent elastic cords," Pole recorded. "One of them appears to be attached to the solar plexus and the other to the brain. As I watch this form it grows more distinct in outline, until I can see that it is an exact counterpart, so far as the form is concerned, of the body on the bed. I can see what looks like spiral currents passing up through these two cords, and as the physical body grows more lifeless, the form hovering above seems to become more vital."

About 40 minutes later, Pole noted that the "double" had become more distinct and that he could see the currents passing through the cords gathering greater momentum. "The life-force is steadily ebbing out of the body, and is apparently passing into the form above."

Some 15 minutes later, Pole observed two figures stoop down over the bed and break the cords at points close to the physical body. "Immediately I see that the form or double rises about two feet from its original position, but remains horizontal, and at this same moment Major P.'s heart stop beating." [5]

Ena Twigg, still another renowned British medium of the last century, reported that she woke with a start one morning to see her sister-in-law, Bea, who was dying of lung cancer in her home some distance away, standing at the foot of her (Twigg's) bed. "I could see the silver cord still attached to her body, so I knew she had not passed," Twigg wrote, adding that she died later that day.

Twigg does not say where or at what distance Bea was from her at the time, but her report is consistent with other reports indicating that the silver cord is so elastic that it can span great distances. [6]

In *Letters from Julia*, published in 1909, William T. Stead*, recorded the following via automatic writing from a woman named Julia Ames, who had died in 1891. Julia informed Stead that she had exchanged experiences with many others on her side of the veil. "With me the change was perfectly painless," Julia wrote through Stead's hand. "I wish that it might be so always with all who are appointed to die. Unfortunately, the moment of transition sometimes seems to be very full of pain and dread. With some it lasts a comparatively long time; I mean the time of quitting the body. With some it is momentary. The envelope opens, the letter is released, and it is over."

Julia likened "death birth" to childbirth, tough for some, relatively simple for others. "The tranquil soul that prepares and knows need not feel even a tremor of alarm," she explained. "The preliminaries of decease are often painful; the actual severance, although sometimes accompanied by a sense of wrench, is of small account."[7]

There have been other reports of difficulties in "giving up the ghost." In *Zeitschrift fuer Parapsychologie*, a clairvoyant man who preferred to remain anonymous reported sitting at his dying wife's bedside and seeing an "odic body" take form over his wife's physical body. It was connected to the physical body by a "cord of od." The arms and legs of this odic body were flailing and kicking as if struggling to get free and escape. Finally, after about five hours, the fatal moment came at last. "There was a sound of gasping," the man reported. "The odic body writhed to and fro, and my wife's breathing ceased. To all appearances she was dead, but a few moments later she began to breathe again. After she had drawn her breath twice, everything became quiet. At the instant of her last breath, the connecting cord broke and the odic body vanished."[8]

One of the earliest accounts of a person's dying moments, as reported by the deceased person himself, was set forth in an 1863 book by Sophia Elizabeth De Morgan, the wife of Augustus De Morgan, the famous mathematician. She reported on the experience of Horace Abraham Ackley, M.D., of Cleveland, Ohio, as communicated through a medium: "I experienced but very little suffering during the last few days of my life, though at first there were struggles, and my features were distorted; but I learned, after my spirit had burst its barriers and was freed from its connection with the external body, that these were produced by it in an attempt to sever this connection, which in all cases is more or less difficult; the vital points of contact being suddenly broken by disease, the union in other portions of the system is necessarily severed with violence, but, as far as I have learned, without consciousness of pain. Like many others, I found that I was unable to leave the form at once. I could feel myself gradually raised from my body, and in a dreamy, half-conscious state. It seemed as though I was not a united being – that I was separated into parts, and yet despite this there seemed to be an indissoluble connecting link. My spirit was freed a short time after the organs of my physical body had entirely ceased to perform their functions. My spiritual form was then united into one, and I was raised a short distance above the body, standing over it by what power I was unable to tell. I could see those who were in the room around me, and knew by what was going on that a considerable time must have elapsed since dissolution had taken place, and I presume I must have been for a time unconscious; and this I find is a common experience, not however, universal." [9]

Communicating through South African trance medium Nina Merrington, Mike Swain, who died in an auto accident, told his father Jasper Swain, a Pietermaritzburg, South Africa lawyer, that he left his body an instant before the cars actually impacted. Heather, his fiancée's young sister, was also killed in the accident. Mike told of being blinded by the glare of the sun reflecting off the windscreen of the oncoming car. "All of a sudden, the radiance changes from silver to gold. I am being lifted up in the air, out through the top of the car. I grab little Heather's hand. She too is being lifted up out of the car." When they were about 30 feet above the car, they witnessed the collision below them and Mike heard a noise like the snapping of steel banjo strings. They had suffered no pain. [10]

Andrew Jackson Davis*, the famous clairvoyant known as the "Poughkeepsie Seer," reported observing many spirit bodies leave the physical body. "I have seen a dying person, even at the last feeble pulse-beat, rouse impulsively and rise up in bed to converse with a friend, but the next instant he was gone – his brain being the last to yield up the life principles," Davis wrote, noting that he often saw a "very fine life-thread" running from the brain and extending up into a golden emanation.

At the Civil War battle of Fort Donelson in 1862, Davis witnessed a soldier blown into many parts by a cannon ball. "I saw that all the particles streamed up and met together in the air," he continued. "The atmosphere was filled with those golden particles – emanations from the dead – over the whole battlefield. About three-quarters of a mile above the smoke of the battlefield – above all the 'clouds that lowered' upon the hills and forests of black discord, there was visible the beautiful accumulation from the fingers and toes and heart and brain of that suddenly killed soldier. There stood the new spiritual body three-quarters of a mile above all the discord and din and havoc of the furious battle! And the bodies of many others were coming up from other directions at the same time." [11]

Many people, both incarnate and discarnate, have reported a mist, smoke, or cloud of some kind over the dying person. Frederic Myers explained that the double hovers above the physical shell for a brief time, during which a "little white cloud" or "pale essence" can be discerned by some.

Eileen Garrett, a renowned medium and clairvoyant, observed a "vital synthetic essence" leave the body of several people as they died, the first when she was a small girl and was present at the death of her cousin. "I became aware of a dim mist that was exuded from her body, weaving intricately within itself in a rhythm that was without agitation, tension, strain, or pressure," she wrote. "Fascinated, I watched the faint small cloud move off into space."

She further witnessed it when her two sons died within a few months of each other. "The dim misty cloud spiraled out from those small bodies as I held them in my arms, and moved away, and with an intensity of desire that was made poignant by my emotional feeling of personal loss, I followed those dim vitalities out and out into endless distances, till the throbbing in my head broke in upon the focus of my concentration."

Later, she observed it with a friend. "I perceived two small clouds emitted from his body – one from the right side of the torso, at the level of the spleen, the other from the top of his head." [12]

Returning to the account given by a German man in *Zeitschrift fuer Parapsychologie,* we read that he also told of being able to see "layers of cloud" drifting into the room as his wife was dying. At first, he assumed it was cigar smoke from an adjoining room and jumped up to express his indignation. "Overcome with wonder, I looked back at the clouds," he reported, commenting that he was completely aware and definitely not imagining what was taking place. "These floated silently toward the bed and enshrouded it completely." He then saw a vaporous body form above his wife's physical body, attached to her body by a vaporous cord. Soon after his wife took her last breath, he observed the cord break and the vaporous body disappear. "I must leave it to the reader to judge whether I was the victim of a hallucination brought on by grief and exhaustion, or whether perhaps my mortal eyes had been privileged to catch a glimpse of the spirit-world in all its happiness, repose, and peace," he ended the report. [13]

Such misty vapors and "lights" around the deathbed have been reported by some psychical researchers, including Dr. Bernard Laubscher, a South African psychiatrist. "I was told by different 'Tant Sannies' (caregivers) how while watching at the bedside of the dying one with one or two candles burning they had seen the formation of a faint vaporous body, an elongated whitish purplish-like cloud; parallel with the dying person and about two feet above the body," Laubscher wrote. "Gradually this cloudlike appearance became denser and took on the form, first vaguely and then more definitely, of the person in the bed. This process continued until the phantom suspended above the body was an absolute replica of the person, especially the face."

Laubscher further recorded that these caregivers, some of whom were apparently clairvoyant, reported seeing a ribbon-like cord stretching from the back of the phantom's head to the body below and that the phantom would begin to glow as it was fully formed.

"They noticed that some were more luminous than others and there was a light all around the outline of the [phantom], which I could only compare to a neon tube," Laubscher added, going on to say that as the phantom righted itself the connecting cord thinned out as if it was fraying away. Sometimes these clairvoyant caregivers would report joyous faces of other deceased gathering around to welcome the person to the spirit world before the "silver cord" was severed and the visions ceased.

As Laubscher came to understand it, the vaporous material has the same makeup as ectoplasm, the mysterious substance given off by physical mediums before materializations. It acts as sort of a "glue" in bonding the physical body with the spirit body, and the more materialistic a person the denser the ectoplasm and the more difficulty the person has in "giving up the ghost." [14]

In the January 25, 1945 issue of *Psychic Observer*, reporter Ed Bodin quoted a young soldier: "I have seen ectoplasm on the battlefield. I have watched it emanate from a badly wounded soldier and then disappear as that soldier breathed his last. One hillbilly comrade from Kentucky called it 'soul mist,' revealing that many natives in his part of the country considered it quite a normal thing, although they seldom talked about it."

Because his orthodox Christian family frowned on discussion of such occult matters, the young soldier asked not to be identified. However, he went on to tell how, after being wounded by shrapnel, another soldier lay badly wounded about 10 feet from him. "I looked at him with pity, forgetting my own pain. Then in the deepening twilight I saw strange smoke begin to curl above him as though coming from his stomach as he lay on his back moaning. The stump of his arm was in the thick mud congealing the blood to some extent and making death slower.

"Then I remembered what my friend had said about soul-mist, and I watched fascinated as the ectoplasm became denser and began to flow toward me. For a moment I thought I saw in it the face of a kindly old lady. Presently it reached me and for a second I was bewildered by the strange sensation that came over me. I felt stronger. With my left arm I raised myself and began to crawl to the dying soldier. I reached for my canteen of water. The mist was still around me, and with a sudden effort I was on my feet, and beside the soldier."

The other soldier died and the young soldier telling the story rose and walked nearly a mile to the Red Cross representative. He remained unconscious for three days and medical attendants later told him that they could not understand how he had lived, to say nothing of walking the near mile to safety. "...to my dying day, I shall believe the ectoplasm from the body of that dying soldier had helped me in a mysterious way," the young soldier added. "It had given me sufficient strength to save my life. That soul-mist of a sacrificed soldier was like the spiritual light of Jesus about whom it was said: 'He could save others, but not Himself'."

George Wehner, a trance medium and clairvoyant from Detroit, Michigan, wrote about his many mediumistic experiences and other paranormal observations, including the passing of his mother. "A misty blue-white form, the counterpart of my mother's, but radiant, like a blue-white diamond's flame, was slowly rising from her body on the bed," he recorded. "This form lifted at an angle, the feet rising higher than the head, which remained attached to the physical head. The form now seemed to try to free itself, and after several tugs, the misty head separated from the body's head, and the freed form righted itself in the air exactly as a log rights itself after it has been dropped into deep water. For a second, I saw several arms and hands materialize in the air and reach downward to welcome the new-born soul. Then, like a shadow, the spirit-form of my beloved mother glided rapidly upward through a corner of the ceiling." [15]

In his 1970 book, *Out of the Body Experiences*, Dr. Robert Crookall quotes Dr. R. B. Hout, a physician who was present at the death of his aunt: "My attention was called...to something immediately above the physical body, suspended in the atmosphere about two feet above the bed. At first I could distinguish nothing more than a vague outline of a hazy, fog-like substance. There seemed to be only a mist held suspended, motionless. But, as I looked, very gradually there grew into my sight a denser, more solid, condensation of this inexplicable vapor. Then I was astonished to see definite outlines presenting themselves, and soon I saw this fog-like substance was assuming a human form."

Hout then saw that the form resembled the physical body of his aunt. The form hung suspended horizontally a few feet above the body. When the phantom form appeared complete, Hout saw his aunt's features clearly. "They were very similar to the physical face, except that a glow of peace and vigor was expressed instead of age and pain. The eyes were closed as though in tranquil sleep, and a luminosity seemed to radiate from the spirit body."

Hout further observed a "silver-like substance" streaming from the head of the physical body to the head of the spirit body. "The colour was a translucent luminous silver radiance. The cord seemed alive with vibrant energy. I could see the pulsations of light stream along the course of it, from the direction of the physical body to the spirit 'double.' With each pulsation the spirit body became more alive and denser, whereas the physical body became quieter and more nearly lifeless..."

When the pulsations of the cord stopped, Hout could see various strands of the cord snapping. When the last connecting strand snapped, the spirit body rose to a vertical position, the eyes opened, and a smile broke from the face before it vanished from his sight.[16]

The Fenwicks devote a chapter of their recent book to "Visions of Light and Mist." They explain that sometimes this grey or white mist, or smoke, will hover above the body before rising to disappear through the ceiling. Some see it, some don't. Among a dozen or more witnesses to this phenomenon, the Fenwicks quote a woman named Penny Bilcliffe, who was present when her sister died: "I saw a fast-moving 'Will 'o the Wisp' appear to leave her body by the side of her mouth on the right. The shock and the beauty of it made me gasp. It appeared like a fluid or gaseous diamond, pristine, sparkly, and pure, akin to the view from above of an eddy in the clearest pool you can imagine...It moved rapidly upwards and was gone." [17]

Gladys Osborne Leonard* told of being at the bedside of a relative as he died. "I noticed that the part of the room in which the bed stood became enveloped in a kind of mist, so that it was isolated or shut off from its surroundings, forming a kind of little world of its own. The outer edge of the mist was roughly circular in form. It was clearest in the centre, immediately round the patient, then became denser toward the edge. It was rather like looking at a scene through a circular window or porthole."

She went on to say that the clearance within the mist was lit by a luminous glow, and within the lighter part of the glow were several human forms. "One of them stood very near the bed, between myself and the patient. Part of the bed was blotted out by the form, which appeared to be opaque. The figure and the face had their back to me, but partly turned to the right so that I saw the profile. It was that of a girl of about eighteen years of age. She was dressed in the old-fashioned manner, of about the 1880s, I guessed...She was bending over the patient in an attentive and expectant manner."

When the vision disappeared, the patient was still breathing, but then Leonard felt a "stillness" creep into the room. "One cannot describe it," she continued. "It is like a complete suspension of everything, as if all life is stopped for a few moments. During it, I heard the breathing going on, but this extraordinary stillness still persisted. I had noticed it on a previous occasion while watching a dying person."

Shortly, the breathing stopped quite suddenly, yet with absolute ease. "There was no gasp or sign of the slightest discomfort, simply a withdrawal...It did not seem like 'death,' that is, as many people visualize death when they think of it as a difficult or painful process, but I knew he had ceased to function in his physical body."

Leonard did not immediately call the nurse, as she was impressed to talk quietly to him, telling him "to dissociate himself from the physical, and give himself entirely into the care of the Spirit-Friends that were around him, with absolute confidence." [18]

In his 2010 book, *Glimpses of Eternity*, Dr. Raymond Moody discusses a "strange mist" that, he noted, is sometimes reported over deathbeds. He explains that some say it looks like smoke, while others see it as more like steam. Some say it seems to have a human shape and that it usually drifts upward before disappearing.

Moody and co-author Paul Perry quote a Georgia doctor who twice saw a mist coming up from deceased patients. The doctor explained that as the patients died they lit up with a bright glow, their eyes shining with a silvery light. The mist formed over the chest and hovered there, as the doctor observed closely and saw that the mist had depth and complex structure. He further said that it seemed to have layers with energetic motion in it. During the second occurrence, the doctor felt an unseen presence standing beside him and seemingly waiting for the patient to die.

A hospice psychologist is quoted by Moody as saying that the misty clouds which form above the head or chest seem to have an electrical component to them. A nurse reported seeing a mist rising from many patients as they die, including her father, with whom she saw the mist rise from his chest, then hover for a few seconds before dissipating.

Moody quotes one man as saying that the room became "uncomfortably bright," so bright that he couldn't shut it out even when he closed his eyes. A hospice nurse reported seeing a luminous presence floating near the bed.

When I reviewed Moody's book at my blog, two people left comments saying that they had witnessed the phenomenon. Ivan B. Cvitan wrote that he was present when a woman died on the beach near his house. He observed a "smoky and lightning something" several meters above the body and had no idea what it was until he read my blog.

Ron Parks of McMinnville, Oregon related a story told to him by someone who had a long career in the timber industry in Oregon. "He told me that once a young man was crushed between two logs in an accident in the woods. They could do nothing for him because of the seriousness of his injuries. As he passed on, they observed a 'mist' rising above his body."

In his best-selling 1916 book, *Raymond or Life and Death*, Sir Oliver Lodge*, in a séance with medium Gladys Osborne Leonard, discussed the subject with Raymond, his deceased son who had been killed on the battlefield in France. Raymond told him that the body doesn't start mortifying until the spirit has left it. He went on to tell his father that he had witnessed a scene several days earlier in which a man was going to be cremated two days after the doctor pronounced him dead. "When his relatives on this side heard about it, they brought a certain doctor on our side, and when they saw that the spirit hadn't got really out of the body, they magnetized it, and helped it out," Raymond explained through Feda, Leonard's spirit control. "But there was still a cord, and it had to be severed rather quickly, and it gave a little shock to the spirit, like as if you had something amputated. But it had to be done."

Raymond suggested that there should be a seven-day waiting period before cremation. "People are so careless," he said. "The idea seems to be 'hurry up and get them out of the way now that they are dead.'" [19]

One of the first psychical researchers was Allan Kardec*, the *nom de plume* of Hippolyte Léon Dénizarth Rivail, a French educator. Among the enlightened spirits purportedly communicating with Kardec through the Boudin sisters, two teenagers, were John the Evangelist, St. Augustine, St. Vincent De Paul, St. Louis, "The Spirit of Truth," Socrates, Plato, Fénelon, Franklin, and Swedenborg. Kardec would meet with one or both of the mediums a couple of evenings every week and put questions to the spirits. The information received by Kardec was said to be well beyond the comprehension of the two mediums. Some of the questions involved the separation of the physical and spirit body, referred to by Kardec as the perispirit. When Kardec asked if separation takes place instantaneously, the communicating spirit responded in the negative. "No, the soul disengages itself gradually," the communication came. "It does not escape at once from the body, like a bird whose cage is suddenly opened. The two states touch and run into each other; and the spirit extricates himself, little by little, from his fleshly bonds, which are loosed, but not broken."

The spirits further explained to Kardec that separation can take place quickly for some, but can take much longer for the "grossly material and sensual." [20]

Many other clairvoyants have suggested that "letting go" or "giving up the ghost" is apparently difficult for many people and depends much upon one's spiritual understanding or, concomitantly, how materialistic the person is. Gladys Osborne Leonard explained that it is sometimes difficult for the etheric body to dissociate itself from the physical envelope. She pointed out that those who lack a spiritual understanding and fear death are more "fixed" in the physical, and thus there is much more of a struggle in the release.

According to Leonard, drinking plenty of water strengthens the etheric body and enables it to more easily separate itself from the physical body. On the other hand, food is not necessary. "Even if they will take it, I am convinced that the dying do not need 'nourishment,' Leonard continued. "To 'nourish' the worn-out physical envelope which the soul is trying its best to shake off is only to create and prolong an unnecessary struggle between the two bodies. In many cases it does not even strengthen the physical, because it can no longer make use of solid food, which only clogs the system, and produces more pain and suffering."

The administration of drugs also hinders an easy transition from the physical to the etheric body, Leonard added, again stressing the need to give the dying person water, even if only a few drops at a time by means of a syringe. "Water is the one thing that the etheric body can make use of when trying to free itself from the physical at the approach of death of the latter."

Keeping the feet warm and a comfortable coolness (not cold or draught) at the head also facilitate, according to Leonard, the withdrawal of the etheric body from the physical.

In helping her husband leave the physical body, Leonard felt drawn by an unseen force to make upward passes from his feet on past his head with her hands. These passes consisted of placing her hands, palms downwards, a few inches above his feet, and moving them steadily and rhythmically over the legs and body, and straight over his head. "At the finish of each pass, I 'flipped' my fingers in a direction away from his body, as if I was throwing off something from my finger-tips," she went on. "Afterwards I learned that that these passes were assisting the etheric body to leave the physical body more easily. It withdraws upwards through the head."

Leonard cautioned against whispered conversations with the nurse in the presence of the dying person, explaining that while the conscious mind may not be cognizant, the unconscious or subjective mind is gradually coming to the surface. This unconscious mind will find itself recording flashes of awareness as to what is happening to the physical body and it will both puzzle and disturb him. "At this juncture it is most important that whatever is being done or said, or even thought in the room, should be directed towards the patient to help him." [21]

In *The Tibetan Book of Living and Dying*, Sogyal Rinpoche discusses the Tibetan tradition called *phowa* (pronounced po-wa), meaning the transference of consciousness. Phowa can be performed by the dying person or by anyone attending the dying person. It involves visualization, meditation, and prayer techniques in which the dying person asks or is asked by those attending to surrender his or her soul to God.

"Sit quietly with the dying person, and offer a candle or light in front of a picture or statue of Buddha or Christ or the Virgin Mary," Rinpoche instructs, after detailing three different practices. "Then do the practice for them. You can be doing the practice quietly, and the person need not even know about it; on the other hand, if he or she is open to it, as sometimes dying people are, share the practice and explain how to do it."

According to Rinpoche and Buddhist teaching, there are two things that count at the moment of death: what we have done during our lives, and what state of mind we are in at the moment. When the consciousness leaves the body, it goes through a series of states called *bardos*." [22]

In *The Challenging Light*, Frances Banks, communicating through the hand of Helen Greaves, states that those making the change from material to ethereal do not recall any pain in the process. "If they experience terror, it is because they *expected* it," explained Banks, an Anglican nun in her earthly life. "The lurid pictures impressed upon the soul-mind by mistaken teachings of hell and torturing agonies become real."

Banks further wrote that her own transition was very simple. She seemed to relapse into *nothingness* until she awoke refreshed. "The death of the human body should hold no terrors," Banks offered, "and when this thought is allowed to be taught and understood by the various practicing religions of the world, a big bogey will have been removed in the onward thinking of the races." [23]

1   Cummins, Geraldine, *The Road to Immortality*, The Aquarian Publishing Co., London, 1932, p. 80

2   Roberts, Estelle, *Fifty Years a Medium*, Gorgi Books, London, 1959, p. 22

3   Myers, F. W. H., *Human Personality and its Survival of Bodily Death*, University Books, New Hyde Park, NY., pp. 212-217

4   Aarons, Marjorie, *The Tapestry of Life*, Psychic Press, Ltd., London, 1979, pg. 27

5   Pole, Wellesley Tudor, *Private Dowding*, Pilgrims Book Service, Norwich, England, 1917, pp. 83-84

6   Twigg, Ena, *Ena Twigg: Medium*, Hawthorne Books, Inc., New York, 1972, p. 168

7   Stead, William T., *Letters From Julia*, The Progressive Thinker Publishing House, Chicago, 1909, pp. 37-38

8   Greber, Johannes, *Communication with The Spirit world of God*, Johanes Greber Memorial Foundation, Teaneck, NJ, 1979, p. 248-249

9   De Morgan, Sophia Elizabeth, *From Matter to Spirit*, Longman, Green Longman, Roberts & Green, London, 1863, pp. 148-149

10 Swain, Jasper, *On the Death of my Son*, Turnstone Press, 1974, p.21

11 Davis, Andrew Jackson, *Death and the After Life*, Colby and Rich, Boston, 1865, pp. 17-18

12 Garrett, Eileen J. *Awareness*, Creative Age Press, Inc., New York, NY, 1943, pp. 149-151

13 Greber, p. 248-249

14 Laubscher, B. J. F., *Beyond Life's Curtain*, Neville Spearman, Jersey, C.I. 1967, pp. 68-70

15 Wehner, George, *A Curious Life*, Horace Liveright, New York, 1929, p. 78

16 Crookall, Robert, *Out of Body Experiences*, Carol Publishing Group., New York, NY., 1970, pp. 153-155

17 Fenwick, Peter & Elizabeth, *The Art of Dying*, Continuum, London, 2008, p. 164

18 Leonard, Gladys Osborne, *The Last Crossing*, Psychic Book Club, London, 1937, pp. 197-199

19 Lodge, Sir Oliver, *Raymond or Life and Death*, George H. Doran Co., New York, 1916, pp. 195-196

20 Kardec, Allan, *The Spirits' Book*, 1855, p. 116

21 Leonard, pp. 40-44

22 Rinpoche, Sogyal, *The Tibetan Book of Living and Dying*, Harper, San Francisco,1994, pp. 223-225

23 Greaves, Helen, *The Challenging Light*, Neville Spearman, Suffolk, UK, 1984, pp. 14-15

4

THE SECOND DEATH &
THE AWAKENING

[My research] *has proven conclusively that death
is only a sleep and an awakening, the process of
awakening depending largely upon the individual's mental attitude, such as religious bias, un-
reasoning skepticism or the willful ignorance of
and indifference to life's meaning, so prevalent
among the multitude.*

— **Carl Wickland, M.D.**

In my years as a competitive long-distance runner, I regularly experienced
the phenomenon referred to as the "second wind." Even for the well-
conditioned runner, the first 150 to 200 yards of a race involves some
stress and struggle as the heart and lungs are asked to suddenly quicken.
However, after around 30 seconds of adjustment, the second wind kicks
in and the body settles down into a relatively effortless rhythm. Whatever
the physiological explanation, this is how I perceived it. It is like a car going through first and second gears before finally shifting into high gear.

As I have come to understand it, the "second death" is something
akin to the second wind. That is, immediately after the silver cord
breaks and the physical body releases the spirit body, i.e., "gives up the
ghost," there is some stress, some confusion, some struggling in the
individual's attempt to adjust to his or her new condition. When the
adjustment is made, the second death is experienced.

Religious references on "second death" are very much muddled and sometimes difficult to reconcile. The term "second death" is found in the New Testament Book of Revelations four times:

2:11: He that hath an ear, let him hear what the spirit saith unto the churches; He that overcometh shall not be hurt of the second death.

20:6: Blessed is he that hath part in the first resurrection; on such the second death has no power, but they shall be priests of God and of Christ, and shall reign with him a thousand years.

20:14: And death and hell were cast into the lake of fire. This is the second death.

21:8: But the fearful and unbelieving, and abominable, and murderers, and whoremongers, and sorcerers, and idolaters, and all liars shall have their part in the lake which burneth with fire and brimstone, which is the second death.

Bible scholars don't agree on the meaning of those verses. They all seem to agree that physical death is the "first" death, but beyond that the interpretations become very convoluted. One popular interpretation puts it that he who has accepted Christ has already died the second death – death to sin. Therefore, it cannot hurt him. Those who actually experience the second death end up in a "lake of fire."

By going beyond the self-imposed limits of orthodox religion, we find a much more logical, more sensible, more inviting environment – one that can be reconciled with a just and loving Creator, and a Divine plan not based on fear. The more metaphysical interpretations – those coming to us from mystics, clairvoyants, and spirit communicators through mediums – make more sense, suggesting that the second death is part of the evolution of spirit in its new environment. In the period immediately following physical death, there is usually some confusion on the part of the spirit and some adjustment or adaptation is required. When this adjustment or adaptation is made, the spirit experiences the second death, thereby settling down in the new environment, much like the long-distance runner adjusts his body rhythm and settles down into a more relaxed effort. For the more spiritually advanced, this adjustment may be a matter of a day or two or three, but for the spiritually challenged, the adjustment may take months or years in earth time.

One mystical teaching holds that the etheric body, or double, is also made up of a "vehicle of vitality," which is shed at the time of the "second death" for an even more subtle body. Different names are given to this third body, but it is referred to here as the "soul body." Some sources suggest a fourth body and a "third death," when the soul sheds yet another body and advances even more.

"We might with justice speak of a first and second death because not only the physical body has to be shed but the next body also," a spirit entity calling himself "Scott" communicated to Jane Sherwood. "Think of the whole man as being composed of four interpenetrating forms. The second of these is very near to the physical in substance and is very closely knit to it. It is the etheric or life-body and gives the power of sensory experience. It never leaves the physical body, even in sleep, but at death it parts from the physical along with the astral and ego bodies. It is too closely related to the physical to allow the higher bodies to pass clearly into their proper sphere, so it also has to be shed and this is the second death." [1]

This transition stage – between the first and second deaths – has been referred to as Hades, which is not synonymous with Hell, as some religions would have us believe. There may be great confusion in Hades, a "fire of the mind," so to speak, by materialistic or spiritually-challenged souls; hence the belief that Hades is the Hell of religion. In effect, Hades seems to be an intermediate or staging area of sorts where the soul must adjust its vibrations to the spirit world. It is said that even Jesus needed a period of adjustment, or at least wanted to experience it so that he knew what others were going through or he wanted to spend some time with them. Thus, he initially spent a day or more in Hades and then on the third day "rose into Heaven." That is, he apparently experienced the second death on the third day. No doubt many fundamentalists have different interpretations.

It may also be that Hades and Paradise are different names for the same staging area, or that Hades is that portion of the staging area reserved for the spiritually-challenged, while Paradise is set aside for the more spiritually advanced. After all, Jesus is said to have told the dying thief on the cross next to him, "Verily I say unto thee, today shalt thou be with me in Paradise." The word Paradise is a Persian word meaning "park" or "resting place."

The spiritually-challenged souls are frequently referred to as "earthbound" spirits, because they have not developed spiritually and cling to earthly ways. The marathon analogy may serve to demonstrate the great differences in time spent in the Hades condition when we liken the spiritually-advanced person to the Olympic marathon runner, who takes a little over two hours to complete the 26.2-mile marathon distance, and the very materialistic person to an overweight "couch-potato," unable to run even a single mile at half the pace of the Olympic athlete. It might take that couch potato years to condition himself to be able to complete the marathon distance, and even then it would me at a much slower pace than that of a well-conditioned runner. If there can be such diversity here on the earth realm in the pursuit of physical excellence, then why not in the pursuit of spiritual consciousness?

Alan Kardec*, the pioneering French psychical researcher, wrote that the confusion following death varies greatly. "It may be only of a few hours, and it may be of several months, or even years," he stated. "Those with whom it lasts the least are they who, during the earthly life, have identified themselves most closely with their future state, because they are soonest able to understand their new situation."

Kardec went on to say that there is nothing painful in this mental confusion for those who have lived an upright life. "He is calm, and his perceptions are those of a peaceful awakening out of sleep. But for him whose conscience is not clean, it is full of anxiety and anguish that become more and more poignant in proportion as he recovers consciousness." [2]

One spirit, referred to by Kardec as a "Mr. Sanson," communicated to Kardec that his state was a very happy one and that he no longer felt the pains he experienced during his final days in the earth life. "The transition from the terrestrial life to the spirit life was, at first, something that I could not understand, and everything seemed incomprehensible to me," Sanson told Kardec, "for we sometimes remain for several days without recovering our clearness of thought; but, before I died, I prayed that God would give me the power of speaking to those I love, and my prayer was granted." He estimated that it took him about eight hours in earth time to regain clearness of thought. [3]

Sanson went on to explain that the instant of death restores to the spirit his normal clairvoyance. That is, the bodily eyes no longer see, but the spirit "sight" is far more penetrating, according to the state of consciousness.

"When I came to myself and was able to look about me, I was dazzled, and could not understand what I saw; for the mind does not regain clearness instantaneously," he continued. "But in proportion, as I recovered the use of my faculties, I perceived that I was surrounded by a numerous company of friends...they were rejoicing in my arrival, and welcomed me with smiles... But what I saw, in my journey through immensity, cannot be described in human speech." [4]

Kardec quoted another spirit relative to what happens to unbelievers: "The confirmed unbeliever experiences, in his last moments, all the anguish of the horrible nightmare in which the sleeper seems to be at the edge of a precipice, on the point of falling into the abyss beneath him. He makes the most agonizing effort to fly from the danger, and he is unable to move; he seeks in vain for something to stay him, some fixed point by which to keep himself out of the terrible void into which he feels himself to be slipping; he tries to call for help and is unable to make any sound. It is under the pressure of this frightful agony that the dying man is seen to writhe in the confusion of the death-throes, wringing his hands, and gasping out stifled and inarticulate cries, all of which are the certain indications of the nightmare from which he is suffering. In ordinary nightmare, your wakening relieves you of the incubus that was oppressing you, and you rejoice to perceive that you have only been dreaming; but the nightmare of death often lasts for a very long time, even for many years, after the separation has taken place; and the suffering thus caused to the spirit is sometimes rendered still more severe by the thick darkness in which he finds himself." [5]

Samuel Philippe, known to Kardec as a very spiritual person when in the flesh, also communicated and told Kardec that although he suffered horribly during his last illness, he underwent no death struggle. "Death came upon me like a sleep, without effort, without any shock," he communicated. "Having no fear of the future, I did not seek to retain my hold upon life, and I had, consequently, no need to struggle against the action of disaggregating. The separation took place without effort, without pain, and even without my knowledge. I am not aware how long this sort of sleep lasted, but it was only for a short time."

Philippe added that he awoke calmly and that it was a delightful contrast to what he had experienced before leaving the body. He felt no pain and rejoiced in his deliverance. However, he was in somewhat of a dazed condition and unable to move. "I gave myself up to it with a sort of enjoyment, without trying to understand my situation, and without having any idea that I had left the earth; everything about me seemed to me like a dream."

Phillippe said that he began to recover his consciousness before his mortal envelope had been buried. He looked upon it with some contempt, congratulating himself that he was rid of it. "The presence of those I had formerly loved filled me with joy; I was not in the least surprised to see them, it appeared to me perfectly natural to do so, but I seemed to have found them again, after a long journey. One thing that surprised me at first [was] that we understood one another without pronouncing a word; our thoughts were transmitted in a single glance, and as though by a sort of fluidic interpenetration." [6]

Emanuel Swedenborg*, the brilliant 17th Century scientist, inventor, and seer, stated: "I have heard from heaven that some people who have died are thinking even while they are lying on the mortuary tables, before their awakening, still within their own cold bodies. As far as they know, they are still alive, except that they are unable to move the smallest bit of matter that belongs to their bodies." [7]

According to Swedenborg, the person's spirit often stays in the body for a while, but not beyond the complete stillness of the heart, which, Swedenborg explained, can continue for quite a long time in some and not so long in others. The moment the heart motion stops, the person is "awakened." This "awakening" means leading a person's spirit out of the physical body and into the spirit world. This, the great seer went on, is what is known as "resurrection."

Whether Swedenborg's "complete stillness of the heart," means the same thing as "clinical death" does today is uncertain, but it does seem that modern medicine is not always certain when a person is really dead, since some people have been revived after being pronounced clinically dead. Swedenborg went on to explain that in his altered state of consciousness he experienced the dying process, at least as far as his physical senses were concerned. His more inward life, including thought, remained unimpaired, so that he perceived and remembered the things that happen to people when they awaken from the dead. "I noticed that [as] physical breathing was almost taken away, the more inward breathing of the spirit kept on, joined to a slight and still breathing of the body," he wrote. "Next, a communication was set up between my heartbeat and the celestial kingdom (since that kingdom corresponds to the heart in man). I even saw angels from there, some at a distance; and two of them were sitting by my head. This resulted in the removal of all my personal affections, although thought and perception continued. I was in this condition for several hours." [8]

Silver Birch, the spirit entity who spoke through the entranced Maurice Barbanell*, said the same thing. "The higher your consciousness, the less the need for adjustment," he communicated. "You must always remember that ours is a mind world, a spirit world where consciousness is king. The mind is enthroned and mind rules. What mind dictates is reality."

Silver Birch added that the time for realization is self-determined. It can be short or long, as measured by our duration of time. For the enlightened, at least those whose actions in the physical world were in accordance with their enlightenment, it is a speedy process.[9]

A very similar message comes from the writings of medium Alice A. Bailey and her teacher, the Tibetan master, Djwhal Khul. They pointed out that most people, being focused on the physical plane, experience a semi-consciousness in the period after death, usually one of emotional and mental bewilderment. "In the case of the [spiritually] undeveloped person, the etheric body can linger for a long time in the neighborhood of its outer disintegrating shell because the pull of the soul is not potent and the material aspect is," we read in *Death: The Great Adventure.* "Where the person is advanced, and therefore detached in his thinking from the physical plane, the dissolution of the vital body can be exceedingly rapid."[10]

As set forth in *No Death: God's Other Door,* Edgar Cayce, the "sleeping prophet," said that "many an individual has remained in that called death for what ye call *years* without realizing it was dead!" Cayce further explained that the "entity" becomes conscious gradually and that this is contingent upon "how great are the appetites and desires of a physical body."[11]

One of the leading psychical investigators in the United States during the early part of the 20th Century was Carl A. Wickland, M.D., whose wife was a trance medium. Wickland recorded the information coming from the spirit world through his wife for some 40 years. "In the case of the open-minded, unbiased individual there is no protracted death sleep, for as transition from the physical draws near he will often discern the presence of waiting friends from the Unseen, bidding him welcome into the new life..." Wickland wrote, going on to state that others may awaken from the death sleep entirely oblivious of their transition and remain in such oblivion for many years as "vagabond spirits."[12]

The Tibetan Book of the Dead refers to this period of awakening as the "Ground Luminosity" or "Clear Light," and says that the vast majority of people do not immediately recognize the Ground Luminosity and are therefore plunged into a state of unconsciousness. As explained by Sogyal Rinpoche, the spiritual director of Rigpa, an international network of Buddhist groups and centers, consciousness continues without the body and goes through a series of states called "bardos." The problem is that in the bardos "most people go on grasping at a false sense of self, with its ghostly grasping at physical solidity, and this continuation of that illusion, which has been at the root of all suffering in life, exposes them in death to more suffering, especially in the 'bardo of becoming'." [13]

Perhaps the "Ground Luminosity" and the "Second Death" both equate to what Westerners call the "light at the end of the tunnel." Many near-death experiencers have reported being in a tunnel and drawn toward the light – a light that emits much love.

Communicating through Geraldine Cummins*, Frederic W. H. Myers* said that he could not generalize as to the conditions in Hades, which he also referred to as the "place of shadows," because conditions varied so much. However, he stated that the "average man who has led a well-ordered life" may very well experience communion with deceased loved ones and see fragmentary happenings of his earthly life, judging himself, before resting, seemingly in a veil while in a state of semi-suspended consciousness. He added that three or four days of earth time may suffice for the Hades experience, but also pointed out that many souls "linger a long while in Hades and wander to and fro in its grim ways, encountering certain strange beings who hover near the borders of the physical world, who wake old sorrows and troubles in the minds of men, and who play upon the understandings of certain individuals they would possess while still in the flesh, dethroning the reason, stealing from man his birthright." [14]

Myers had died, at age 57, on January 17, 1901 while in Rome. The first communication from him came through Rosalie Thompson, a medium, to Professor Oliver Lodge* and his wife on February 19, 1901. However, it was clear that Myers was struggling to communicate. He told the Lodges that he was confused when he first arrived on the other side, before he realized he was dead. "I thought I had lost my way in a strange town, and I groped my way along the passage," he said. "And even when I saw people that I knew were dead, I thought they were only visions. I have not seen Tennyson yet by the way."

Myers continued, explaining that in attempting to visualize the surroundings at the Lodge home during the sitting, it was if he were looking at a misty picture. He could hear himself using Thompson's voice, but he didn't feel like it was his "whole self" talking. He said he was having a difficult time in remembering things. In fact, he could not recall his mother's name. When Lodge asked him about the Society for Psychical Research, of which Myers was a cofounder, Myers could not recall anything about the organization. Nelly, the medium's spirit control, took over the medium's entranced mechanism and explained that Myers was still in a state of confusion and would remember a great deal more in time. [15]

Over and over again, the messages have come saying that awareness or consciousness on that side of the veil is in proportion to the spiritual awareness or consciousness while on earth. There are some who immediately recognize that they have departed the earth life, while others are slow to understand their condition. "I awoke standing by my dead body, thinking I was still alive and in my ordinary physical frame," Julia Ames communicated to William T. Stead*. "It was only when I saw the corpse in the bed that I knew that something had happened." [16]

Stead, who was very much involved with Spiritualism, was a victim of the *Titanic* disaster in 1912. One survivor recalled Stead sitting calmly in the smoking room while apparently reading a Bible as chaos gripped nearly everyone else on the ship. Not long after his death, Stead began communicating through a number of mediums in both Great Britain and the United States. Communicating to his daughter, Estelle, Stead recalled that his first awareness that he had passed over was when he found a number of deceased friends with him. "I knew it suddenly and was a trifle alarmed," he communicated. "Practically instantaneously I found myself looking for myself. Just a moment of agitation, momentarily only, and then the full and glorious realization that all I had learnt was true."

All of the victims seemed to gather in one place as their bodies floated in the ocean below. Some of them were mental wrecks, wondering if they would be taken to meet their Maker and what their sentences would be, while others were more concerned with loved ones left behind. There were a number, however, who seemed more concerned about their valuables that went down with the ship.

After all of the victims gathered together, they seemed to rise vertically into the air at a terrific speed, as if they were all standing on a platform. "I cannot tell how long our journey lasted, nor how far from the earth we were when we arrived, but it was a gloriously beautiful arrival. It was like walking from your own English winter gloom into the radiance of an Indian sky. There was all brightness and beauty."

After their arrival, they were greeted by many old friends and relatives and then all parted company. Stead's father then accompanied him to a temporary rest home, which he was told was for newly-arrived spirit people. "It was nearest to earth conditions and was used because it resembled an earth place in appearance," Stead explained his arrival in what seems to have been the Hades condition, going on to say that the main objective was to get rid of unhappiness at parting from earth ties.

"On arriving here there is often much grief," Stead continued. "Grief that is sometimes incapacitating, and no movement forward can be made until the individual wishes it himself. Progress cannot be forced upon him." [17]

A spirit identifying himself as Thomas Dowding, a schoolmaster who joined the British army and was then killed on the battlefield, communicated to Wellesley Tudor Pole that one moment he was alive and the next moment he was helping two of his friends carry his body down the trench labyrinth. "I did not know whether I had jumped out of my body through shell shock, temporarily or for ever," he told Pole. "You see what a small thing is death, even the violent death of war! I seemed in a dream...Death for me was a simple experience – no horror, no long-drawn suffering, no conflict. It comes to many in the same way."

Dowding said he experienced no pain when struck by a shell splinter. After his body was taken to the field mortuary, he remained near it the entire night, expecting to wake up in the body again. He then lost consciousness. When he awoke the next morning, his body was gone and he began hunting for it. He then realized that he must be dead. Once he recovered from the shock of that realization, he felt as if he were floating in a mist that muffled sound and blurred the vision. "It was like looking through the wrong end of a telescope. Everything was distant, minute, misty, unreal. Guns were being fired. It might all have been millions of miles away...I think I fell asleep for the second time, and long remained unconscious and in a dreamless condition."

When he "awoke" the second time, he felt cramped, but this feeling gradually left him. "I think my new faculties are now in working order," he continued his story. "I can reason and think and feel and move."

Dowding was welcomed by his brother, William, who had died three years earlier, and accompanied to a rest hall. William explained to him that it took some time for him to help him because the atmosphere was so thick. "He hoped to reach me in time to avert the 'shock' to which I have referred, but found it impossible." It was after reaching the rest hall that things became clearer and he was no longer confused. [18]

The Spiritualist classic, *Claude's Book*, relates communication between Claude, a British pilot killed when shot down by the Germans in World War I, and his mother through the trance mediumship of Gladys Osborne Leonard*. Early on, Claude explained his passing. He first felt a blow on his head, a sensation of dizziness and falling, and then nothing more. "It may have been a fortnight or more later that I became conscious again," he told his mother through Leonard, further commenting that he had no account of time there, so he could not be sure.

After he became fully conscious on the other side, Claude received an orientation and was then put to work greeting other casualties of the war. "We bring them away so that they may return to consciousness far from their mutilated physical bodies, and oh, Mum, I feel quite tired sometimes of explaining to men that they are *dead*. They wake up feeling so much the same; some go about for days, and even months, believing they are dreaming."[19]

Young Mike Swain, killed along with his fiancé's young sister, in a head-on auto collision, communicated to his father that he immediately found his Uncle Mark standing next to him. "He explained that we had been through such a terrible collision that we were no longer in the land of the living," Mike said. "I was too surprised to ask him how he knew, although I did have a hunch I was dead, and it seemed perfectly natural that he had come to take charge of us. I decided that Heather and I couldn't do better than go along with him, so we did…I can't say exactly how long it took us to leave the earth plane. It was rather much like flipping a radio dial from one station to another. When you turn the knob, you take for granted that another station will be awaiting your pleasure; you don't think there's anything unusual about it. That was how we moved from your world to our new one. All our family, even the ones we didn't know when we were on the earth, were here to welcome us. They made us feel wanted and very much at home."

Mike went on to explain that in order for him to communicate through the medium, he had to reduce his vibrations to their slowest rate. "This isn't easy, Dad; some of it is downright painful. It's like putting on a straight-jacket. I have to constrict myself more and more, like the rabbit in *Alice in Wonderland,* until my vibrations are moving as slowly as yours."[20] He went on to say that he had discovered that he was one of few people who could so lower his vibrations, and that perhaps 95 percent of the souls there are unable to manifest at the earth level.

Many spirit communicators have said that the grief and sorrow of loved ones left behind prevented them from awakening. "The spirit body may take some days of your time before it becomes completely separated from the earthly body, and it may be hindered very much by the combined thoughts of the sorrowers who are participants in the dismal rites," the discarnate Monsignor Robert Hugh Benson communicated through Anthony Borgia. "Instead of departing from the earthly sphere, the discarnate one will be attracted to the scene of [funeral and memorial] activities, and more than likely will be saddened himself by what he is witnessing and by the sorrow of those left behind." [21] Benson added that those in the spirit world would like to see the complete abolition of such funeral rites which talk about "eternal rest" or are otherwise filled with doom and gloom.

The Rev. William Stainton Moses*, an Anglican minister and university English instructor, scoffed at mediumship until he discovered that he, himself, was a medium. A spirit calling himself Imperator communicated seemingly higher truths through Moses by means of automatic writing. At one sitting, Moses inquired about the fate of a spirit who was known to be impious, disobedient, heedless, idle, and selfish. "When the cord of earth-life was severed, the spirit found itself in darkness and distress," Imperator related. "For long it was unable to sever itself from the body. It hovered round it even after the grave had closed over the shrine which it had violated. It was unconscious, without power of movement, weak, wounded, and distressed. It found no rest, no welcome in the world to which it had come unbidden. Darkness surrounded it, and through the gloom dimly flitted the forms of congenial spirits who had made shipwrecks of themselves, and were in unrestful isolation. These drew near, and their atmosphere added vague discomfort to the half-conscious spirit."

Imperator went on to explain that ministering spirits were there to attempt to awaken him. By showing him the error of his ways, they hoped to create in him proper remorse, but the spirit initially resisted. By degrees they succeeded in awakening some measure of consciousness in him and the spirit began to grope blindly for some means of escape. Frequent relapses dragged it back as tempters were all around him.

"This is the inevitable penalty of a wasted life," Imperator continued. "It may be that the half-quenched spark may be quickened again, and be fanned into a flame strong enough to light the spirit onward. It may be that the spirit may wander in gloom and desolation, deaf to the voices of the ministers, and groaning in lonely unrest, nerveless for the struggle, till the sin through cycles of purgatorial suffering, has eaten out its virulence." [22]

The bottom line here seems to be that the moral state of the individual determines the ease with which he or she "gives up the ghost" and then "awakens" on the Other Side.

[1] Sherwood, Jane, *The Country Beyond*, Neville Spearman, London, 1969, p. 61

[2] Kardec, Allan, *The Spirits' Book*, 1855, pg. 119

[3] Kardec, Allan, *Heaven and Hell*, Trubner & Co., London, 1878, pp. 202-203

[4] _____ p. 208

[5] _____ p. 207

[6] _____ p. 221-222

[7] Swedenborg, Emanuel, *Heaven & Hell*, Swedenborg Foundation, West Chester, PA., 1976, p. 338

[8] _____ p. 345

[9] Naylor, William, *Silver Birch Anthology*, Spiritualist Press, London, 1955, p. 59.

[10] Bailey, Alice A., Death: *The Great Adventure*, Lucis Press Ltd., London, 1985, pp. 37-38

[11] Cayce, Edgar, *"No Death: God's Other Door*, A. R. E. Press, Virginia Beach, VA, 1998, p.48

[12] Wickland, Carl E., *The Gateway of Understanding*, Nat. Psychological Instit. Los Angeles, 1934, p. 16

[13] Rinpoche, Sogyal, *The Tibetan Book of Living and Dying*, Harper San Francisco, 1993, p. 242

[14] Cummins, Geraldine, *The Road to Immortality*, The Aquarian Press, London, 1955, pp. 82-83

[15] Lodge, Oliver, *The Survival of Man*, Moffat, Yard and Company, New York, 1909, p. 344

[16] Stead, William T., *Letters from Julia*, The Progressive Thinker Publishing House, Chicago, 1909, p. 38

[17] Stead, Estelle, *The Blue Island*, Hutchinson & Co., London, 1922, pp. 35-38

[18] Pole, Wellesley Tudor, *Private Dowding*, The Thetford Press Ltd., Norfolk UK, 1917, pp. 15-18

[19] Kelway-Bamber, L., *Claude's Book*, Psychic Book Club, London, p. 11

[20] Swain, Jasper, *On the Death of my Son*, Turnstone Press, 1974, pp.54-55

[21] Borgia, Anthony, *Here and Hereafter*, H. G. White, San Francisco, 1968, p. 28

[22] Moses, William Stainton, *Spirit Teachings*, London Spiritualist Alliance, 1924, pp.274-276.

5

THE LIFE REVIEW

*God is not mocked; whatever a man soweth that
shall he also reap.*

— **Galatians 6:71**

After many years of murdering, raping, plundering, and pillaging
with malice and forethought, twin brothers Jed and Ned were finally stopped by the police. Jed was shot and killed instantly, while
Ned was apprehended and sent to prison for life. During his confine-
ment, Ned "found" God and repented.

Jed and Ned are fictional characters created here to examine divine
justice as perceived by biblical orthodoxy. The predominant view is
that Jed faces eternal torment in hell, while Ned has been "saved" and
will experience everlasting bliss in heaven, assuming, of course, that
he found the "right" God and showed proper remorse.

One "school" holds that both Jed and Ned will "sleep" until some
far-off Judgment Day when their moldering bodies will be restored and
raised from their graves so that they can then receive appropriate sentences imposed by God or a high tribunal. Another school has them
being judged soon after death and occupying their new environments
almost immediately, although with Catholics there is an intermediate
state called purgatory in which sins must be purged before one is allowed entrance to heaven. Purgatory is purportedly as bad as hell but
not eternal.

In between those two views, there is one in which there is something of "double judgment." The soul is judged soon after death and sent to what might be called a staging area while awaiting a final judgment on the day or resurrection. Exactly how the second judgment differs from the first judgment no religious authority seems to know. Simon Tugwell, an Oxford theologian, suggests that this double judgment is a fundamental ambiguity and an embarrassment to the Christians who accept it, but may be so only because humans are unable to comprehend the timelessness of the afterlife.

In the case of Jed and Ned and countless others, it seems that luck is a big factor in determining one's salvation, or destiny, in the afterlife, irrespective of which of the belief systems he or she subscribes to. Clearly, Jed was the unlucky one in catching the bullet, while Ned lucked out by avoiding the bullet. When orthodox leaders are asked to explain why God allows luck to play a part in one's ultimate destiny, the scripted answer is that we are incapable of understanding or knowing God's ways. In the great scheme of things, justice prevails, they assert with great conviction, even if we are unable to comprehend it.

But not all believers are dogmatically fixed in their view of how judgment is meted out in the afterlife. According to Michael J. Taylor, a professor emeritus of religious studies at Seattle University in Washington, a new theology of death has emerged. Instead of God passing judgment as the person stands passively before Him, the dying person is allowed to make a final choice for or against God. In effect, the person chooses an eternity with or without God. Apparently, the person does not see the latter state as the horrific hell of orthodoxy, but rather as one of self-love. His decision is based upon what he has learned during his lifetime. If he does not opt for an eternity with God, then he must surely be in for a rude awakening.

However, modern revelation, coming to us primarily through mediumship, the near-death experience (NDE), and various forms of mysticism, suggests a life review or self-judgment, if it can be called a "judgment." It further suggests that there are many levels in the afterlife environment and that we automatically go to a certain level based on what might be called a "moral specific gravity."

Many NDErs have reported a "life review" in which they see definitive moments in their life flash before them during the experience. P. M. H. Atwater, whose NDE took place during 1977, reported that she saw every thought she had ever had, every word she had ever spoken, and every deed she had ever done during her life review. Moreover, she saw the effects of every thought, word, and deed on everyone who might have been affected by them. As she interpreted it, she was judging herself.

Tom Sawyer, who had an NDE in 1978 when his car fell on him while he was working under it, recalled reliving every thought and attitude connected with decisive moments in his life and seeing them through the eyes of those who were affected by his actions. He particularly recalled an incident that took place when he was driving his hot-rod pickup at age 19 and nearly hit a jaywalking pedestrian who darted in front of him from behind another vehicle. When Sawyer engaged in a verbal exchange with the pedestrian, the man yelled some four-letter words at him, reached through the window, and hit him with his open hand. Sawyer responded by jumping out of his car and beating the man relentlessly. During his life review, Sawyer came to know everything about the man, including his age, the fact that his wife had recently died, and that he was in a drunken state because of his bereavement.

Sawyer came to see the attack from his victim's standpoint. "[I experienced] seeing Tom Sawyer's fist come directly into my face, and I felt the indignation, the rage, the embarrassment, the frustration, the physical pain...I felt my teeth going through my lower lip – in other words, I was in that man's eyes. I was in that man's body. I experienced everything of that inter-relationship between Tom Sawyer and that man that day. I experienced unbelievable things about that man that are of a very personal, confidential, and private nature." [1]

In his recent book, *Evidence of the Afterlife*, Jeffrey Long, M.D. quotes a young woman who nearly died from a complication of anesthesia: "My entire consciousness seemed to be in my head. Then I started seeing pictures. I think they were in color. It was as if someone had started a movie of myself and of my entire life, but going backwards from the present moment...This panoramic review of my life was very distinct; every little detail of the incidents, relationships, was there – the relationships in some sort of distilled essence of meaning..." [2]

Long also tells of a man named Roger who was in a head-on auto accident and immediately left his body. He told of seeing events from above: "I went into a dark place with nothing around me, but I wasn't scared. It was really peaceful there. I then began to see my whole life unfolding before me like a film projected on a screen, from babyhood to adult life. It was so real! I was looking at myself, but better than a 3-D movie as I was also capable to sensing the feelings of the persons I had interacted with through the years. I could feel the good and bad emotions I made them go through..." [3]

Pseudoskeptics seem to have a theory for every aspect of the NDE, including the life review which so many others have reported. The "skeptical" take on the life review is that it is a psychological defense mechanism permitting a retreat into pleasant memories. But Long points out that many memories are not pleasant and that such unpleasant memories would not be expected in a psychological escape. Certainly, it was not pleasant for Tom Sawyer to be on the receiving end of his own blows.

Long further mentions the "Oprah Factor," which suggests that people, upon reading or hearing of these reports, are conditioned to make up such stories. However, a number of dynamic NDEs with life reviews can be found in print well before Dr. Raymond Moody gave a name to it and popularized it in his 1975 book, *Life After Life.* In an 1863 book, author Sophia Elizabeth De Morgan, the wife of the renowned British mathematician and logician Augustus De Morgan, relates what was obviously an NDE by British Rear Admiral Sir Francis Beaufort (1774-1857), who is most remembered today for devising the Beaufort Wind Scales. The experience took place sometime around 1795, when he was a young sailor on one of His Majesty's ships in Portsmouth harbor. Beaufort wrote that he was sculling about in a small boat endeavoring to fasten the boat to a ship when he stepped upon the gunwale, lost his balance, and fell into the water. Not knowing how to swim, he splashed about before he began to sink below the surface and drown. After experiencing "perfect tranquility," he had his life played back before him. "They took, then, a wider range: our last cruise – a former voyage and shipwreck – my school, the progress I had made there, the time I had misspent, and even all my boyish pursuits and adventures," Beaufort wrote. "Thus, traveling backwards, every incident of my past life seemed to me to glance across my recollection in retrograde procession; *not, however, in mere outline as here stated,* but the picture filled up with every minute and collateral feature; in short, the whole period of my existence seemed to be placed before me in a kind of panoramic view, and each act of it seemed to be accompanied by a consciousness of right or wrong, or by some reflection on its cause of consequence – indeed many trifling events, which had been long forgotten, then crowded into my imagination, and with the character of recent familiarity." [4]

Beaufort then speculated on the meaning of it all, wondering if it was some indication of the almost infinite power of memory with which we awaken in another world. "But however that may be, one circumstance was highly remarkable, that the innumerable ideas which floated into my mind were all retrospective; yet I had been religiously brought up; my hopes and fears of the next world had lost nothing of their early strength, and at any other period intense interest and awful anxiety would have been excited by the mere idea that I was floating on the threshold of eternity; yet at that inexplicable moment, when I had full consciousness that I had already crossed that threshold, not a single thought wandered into the future; I was wrapped entirely in the past. The length of time that was occupied by this deluge of ideas, or rather the shortness of time into which they were condensed, I cannot now state with precision; yet, certainly, two minutes could not have elapsed from the moment of suffocation to the time of my being hauled up." [5]

It would be difficult to find a more credible person than Carl Gustav Jung, the eminent Swiss psychiatrist, who experienced an NDE in 1944 after breaking his foot and then having a heart attack. He recalled his experience: "It was as if I now carried along with me everything I had ever experienced or done, everything that had happened around me," he wrote. "I might also say: it was with me, and I was it. I consisted of all that, so to speak. I consisted of my own history, and I felt with great certainty: this is what I am. 'I am this bundle of what has been, and what has been accomplished.'" [6]

Jung went on to say that he felt certain that he was about to enter an illuminated room and then understand the historical nexus of his life and what would come after. However, his vision ceased as he returned to earthly consciousness.

But how can a person see every moment of his life flash before him in an instant? As Pim Van Lommel, a renowned Dutch cardiologist, understands it, many aspects of the NDE correspond with or are analogous to some of the basic principles from quantum theory, which is non-local, i.e., timeless and placeless interconnectedness. Or to view it another way, consciousness outside of the objective world is independent of time.

The Rev. William Stainton Moses*, an Anglican priest, developed the ability to communicate with spirits and put many questions to an apparently advanced spirit called Imperator. Moses often had a difficult time reconciling what Imperator had to say with the teachings of the Church. In response to a question about a Judgment Day, Imperator replied: "Is it nothing that we tell you that reward and punishment are not delayed till a far-off day faintly imagined, after a period of torpor, almost of death, but are instant, immediate, supervening upon sin by the action of an invariable law, and acting ceaselessly until the cause which produced it is removed?" [7]

Moses also asked about a General Judgment, to which Imperator replied there was no such thing but that judgment is ceaseless as the soul is forever evolving. He further stated that an arraignment before an assembled universe is an allegory. "The judgment is complete when the spirit gravitates to the home which it has made for itself. There can be no error. It is placed by the eternal law of fitness. That judgment is complete until the spirit is fitted to pass to a higher sphere, when the same process is repeated, and so on and on until the purgatorial spheres of work are done with, and the soul passes within the inner heaven of contemplation." [8]

After his death in 1901, pioneering psychical researcher Frederic W. H. Myers* communicated extensively through several mediums, including Geraldine Cummins of Ireland. He said that following death the soul experiences a semi-suspended consciousness during which it sees fragmentary happenings of the life just lived. "He watches this changing show as a man drowsily watches a shimmering sunny landscape on a midsummer day. He is detached and apart, judging the individual who participates in these experiences, judging his own self with aid of the Light from Above." [9]

Myers further explained that while this is taking place, the etheric or spirit body is loosening itself from the "husk" and when the judgment is completed, generally after three to four days, the soul takes flight and resumes full consciousness. However, he added that some men and women "linger" a much longer time in the Hades condition wandering to and fro in grim ways.

Communicating to Marjorie Aarons through the direct-voice mediumship of the renowned British medium Lilian Bailey, Bill Wootton said that everyone is his or her own judge and jury. "There is nobody sitting in awful majesty weighing this on the one hand and that on the other. When you are out of the physical body with its limiting brain and five senses, you have a greater horizon of thought which is immediately stimulated by the knowledge that you are alive. But you see with an awful clarity the smallness of what you were, yet somehow you have an immense feeling of being more powerful. The first thing you want to do is to try to rectify some things you definitely made into a mess...You try to inspire or help where you have left some things undone. Very often we are all apt to see these as bigger than they actually were." [10]

Wootton went on to say that some souls remain in a state of not wishing to know for many years and continue to suffer the torments of their conscience. Eventually, however, they are urged to rise above that condition.

Jane Sherwood, a British automatic writing medium, received messages from a spirit referred to as "E.K." In describing his own transition, E. K. said the he found himself awake but that his body was no longer frail and weak as it had been before passing. His thoughts turned inward and moved at a surprising rate. "It raced over the record of a long lifetime which it lit up with a searchlight that spared no blunders, sins or weaknesses, but impartially illumined it all, as one holds up an old, finished garment to the light and notes with dismay its rents and stains. This clear breeze of recollection showed me the honest shape and cut of the thing too. I reviewed it as though I had no longer a special responsibility for it but had to understand clearly in what it had failed and in what succeeded." [11]

The student of mediumistic phenomena comes to realize that reports from the afterlife are filtered through the brain of the medium and therefore are couched in her or his words, sometimes distorted, but generally delivering the gist of what the communicating spirit attempts to deliver. These spirits often explain that terrestrial language is inadequate for them to describe their environment and experiences. Communicating through the hand of Mrs. E. B. Duffey, a "dear friend" of hers put it this way: "How can I describe to you that which has no parallel on earth? I can give you an imperfect idea of what now occurred, though it came to me with a force hitherto unparalleled in either my earthly or my spiritual existence. The air seemed filled with a strange murmur, and clouds descended and shut from my view all outward objects...The story of my life was being told in tones that, it seemed to me, must reach to the farthest heavens, and its events were pictured before me by the tossing clouds. I use the words heard and saw, and yet I am not sure that I did either. But the impression made upon my mind was as if all senses had united in one grand effort to place my past life in its true phases before me. I sat appalled and dismayed, and then as the record of weaknesses and failures went on, I covered my face with my hands and sank in agony and shame to the ground...I summoned all my courage, and since I must sit in judgment on myself, I resolved to do so bravely and thoroughly. How many sombre pictures there were! How many half light, half shade; but now and then there was a bright one in which some unconscious unselfishness, some little deed I had done and forgotten, without any thought of secret self-glorification, and which had not only been good in its results, but which has sprung from a fountain of genuine good within my heart, shone out like a jewel from the dark clouds which surrounded it." [12]

It is somewhat difficult to reconcile the seemingly immediate life review of the near-death experiencer with the delayed life review of the mediumship reports. It may be that the NDE life review is a preview of some kind given to a person who is returning to his physical body so that he or she can learn from it. It may also be that we have many life reviews in the early stages. But it could also be the non-local aspect of time in the spirit world. Hilda, the sister-in-law of Geraldine Cummins*, explained it this way: "So far as my knowledge goes, [the judgment] does not take place on our immediate arrival here. The word 'day' is incorrect, for the trial is not limited to twenty-four hours. It is not possible to talk of it in terms of earth-time. But there is a special period when we enter the Gallery of Memory and the pictures of our earth-life pass before us one by one. Then our own spirit is our judge. We face this time when we are fit for it, when the wounds received during our journey on earth have been healed. I haven't been up for Judgment yet." [13]

Hilda added that no two people have exactly the same experiences because no two souls are exactly alike. The discarnate William James said much the same thing through the automatic writing of Jane Roberts, pointing out that each individual will interpret the experience according to his or her own beliefs and characteristics. James communicated: "It is impossible to tell how long this takes in earth terms, but the inner dimensions of the experience are equally beyond description, for there is nothing in life to compare with the depth, breadth, complexity, or intensity of such a psychological multievent." [14]

Perhaps this also explains why only a small percentage of people who have had a near-death experience report a life review. In his 2008 book, *To Die For*, physicist James Beichler offers a theory of death which encompasses many things learned from paranormal phenomena, including near-death experiences, mysticism, astral travel, and mediumship. He speculates that a person who has a highly-developed spiritual consciousness – one that has kept pace with the development of the mind – may not need a life review as the person has reviewed his or her life when alive in the flesh. At the other extreme, there are those not advanced enough in their conscious evolution to appreciate a life review, and still others who may not accept a life review because they deny their death and sense nothing at all. "In other words, people's minds seize upon the most familiar surroundings when they enter the new environment of the five-dimensional universe, but can still reject the experience completely depending upon their mind set and mental priorities at the time of death," Beichler surmises.[15]

Sometime in 1892, Edward C. Randall, a prominent Buffalo, New York trial lawyer and businessman, was asked by a friend to accompany him on a visit to Emily S. French, a Rochester woman who, Randall was told, had strange powers and received messages from spirits by means of the direct-voice method of mediumship. Over the next 20 years, Randall sat with French more than 700 times, recording the messages from various spirits. He pointed out that each voice had individuality and that they varied greatly, just as they do in earth life. One such voice reported: "Every thought, being material, creates a condition about us and is retained in the brain. When, therefore, anyone goes out of this life and enters the etheric, where everything, the good and the bad, is intensified beyond measure, the storehouse of the brain is opened and he is confronted with the record made. Nothing is forgotten." [16]

In 1853, Dr. Robert Hare, a renowned inventor and an emeritus professor of chemistry at the University of Pennsylvania medical school, commenced an investigation of mediums with the intent of debunking them. However, he was soon converted to Spiritualism and received many messages from the spirit world explaining how things operated on that side. As he came to see it, one's immediate place in the afterlife is determined by a sort of "moral specific gravity."

This moral specific gravity is apparently built up during a person's lifetime based on his or her good works or lack thereof and manifests itself in the person's energy field, or aura. Hare called it a circumambient halo and was told that it passes from darkness to effulgence based on the degree of spiritual advancement. Moreover, one cannot be dishonest with himself as the moral specific gravity allows him to tolerate only so much light. If he were to try to cheat and go to a higher plane, he would not be able to tolerate the light there.

As Hare and others accepting the philosophy of Spiritualism came to understand it, the afterlife is made up of many planes, spheres, realms, states, or, as Jesus is quoted, "many mansions in my Father's house." The person with a low moral specific gravity will gravitate to a low plane, but can still be enlightened and gradually evolve to a higher plane with the help of more enlightened spirits or by means of prayer from those still incarnate. Those accepting reincarnation see the moral specific gravity being imprinted on the person's energy field and playing itself out as *karma*.

As discussed in prior chapters, Emanuel Swedenborg* reported extensively on his visits into the afterlife environment. He wrote: "The details which a person has thought, intended, said, done – even what he has heard and seen – are written on his inner or spiritual memory...the spirit is formed in keeping with the thoughts and acts of its intention." [17]

Andrew Jackson Davis* put it this way in his 1865 book: "The theory that all people will sometime go before the bar of God, and that there is a systematic heavenly tribunal, is the sheerest fancy of a materialistic theology. Both God and Nature are with you at all times. The interior principle of Justice, whether you know it or not, is the ever-present 'bar of God' at which you are arraigned and tried, and deathless Memory is 'the accusing angel.' It gives you the document setting forth your exculpation; or else it explains to you, beyond controversy, the all-sufficient grounds for your condemnation." [18]

Davis further stated that the person "gravitates" to a particular sphere or plane in the afterlife environment based on this "memory." He added that persons who have committed involuntary wrong do not suffer from the same *internal oppression* as those who do voluntary wrong.

After Mike Swain was killed in an auto accident, he began communicating with his father, Jasper Swain, a South African lawyer, through a medium. At one sitting, he communicated: "Dad, everyone comes here through the gates of death. You have to re-arrange your values to appreciate its virtues, though! While you are still on earth, your thought – your intentions – every thing you do – gives your soul a certain rate of vibration. For argument's sake, let's suppose your soul is vibrating in a fifty megacycle band. When you die and manifest here, you would go straight to the part of our world which vibrates at fifty megacycles. By the same token, if you're a slow-thinking sort of bloke who can only vibrate to fifteen megacycles, then you'll become part of this world in the fifteen megacycle range. It all depends on your rate of vibration, see?" [19]

Seemingly consistent with this moral specific gravity and vibrational ideas is the explanation given to Frederick C. Schulthorp during his early 20th Century astral projections. Schulthorp was told by spirits he encountered during his astral travels that every thought generates an electrical impulse that is impressed upon the individual's energy field and is stored there. Every thought, they explained, has a specific rate of vibration. The combined vibrations over a lifetime determine the person's initial station in the afterlife environment. At a time before computer chips made this comprehensible, Schulthorp expressed his understanding this way: "Upon entry into spirit life, a person will naturally and automatically gravitate to his state in spirit which corresponds to his acts and thoughts throughout life as reproduced by his 'personal tape record.'"[20]

As he further understood, a person whose inner nature was friendly and considerate to others during earth life would automatically gravitate to the same wavelength in spirit, even if that person had been ignorant of spirit or religion. And that spirit would not be separated from relations and friends not so progressed as the higher can always go to the lower.

The dichotomous afterlife of most of orthodoxy suggests that we are judged either righteous or wicked, no middle ground whatsoever. Moreover, the vicarious atonement of Christianity only convolutes the idea and adds even greater injustice to it. A multi-faceted afterlife, one consisting of many planes, spheres, realms, levels, abodes, or "mansions," as further discussed in the next chapter, is consistent with the gravitational lessons coming to us through modern revelation. It is likely that the purgatory of Catholicism resulted from early Church leaders recognizing some kind of middle ground, even if they did not see it as multi-layered.

A "moral specific gravity" with "many mansions" is an idea that appeals to reason and one that can be reconciled with a just and loving God. It is a plan of attainment and attunement, of gradual spiritual growth, and of reaping what we sow.

[1] Farr, Sidney Saylor, *What Tom Sawyer Learned from Dying*, Hampton Roads Publishing Co., Ltd., Norfolk, VA, 1993, p. 33

[2] Long, Jeffrey, M.D., *Evidence of the Afterlife*, Harper-Collins, New York, NY, 2010, p. 48

[3] _____ p. 111

[4] De Morgan, Sophia Elizabeth, *From Matter to Spirit*, Longman, Green, Longman, Roberts, & Green, London, 1863, p. 179

[5] _____ pp. 180-182

[6] Jung, C. G., *Memories, Dreams, Reflections*, Vintage Books, New York, NY, 1989, p. 291

[7] Moses, William Stainton, *Spirit Teachings*, London Spiritualist Alliance, London, 1924, p. 21

[8] _____ p. 227

9 Cummins, Geraldine, (I) *The Road to Immortality*, The Aquarian Press, London, 1955, p. 82

10 Aarons, Marjorie, *The Tapestry of Life*, Psychic Press Ltd., London, 1979, p. 56

11 Sherwood, Jane, *The Country Beyond*, Neville Spearman, London, 1969, p. 63

12 Duffey, Mrs. E. B., *Heaven Revised*, Two Worlds Publishing Co., Manchester, UK, 1921, p. 26

13 Cummins, Geraldine, (II), *Travelers in Eternity*, Psychic Press, Ltd., London, 1948, p. 20

14 Roberts, Jane, *The Afterdeath Journal of an American Philosopher*, Prentice-Hall, Inc., Englewood Cliffs, NJ, 1978, p. 120

15 Beichler, James E., *To Die For*, Trafford Publishing, Victoria, B.C., 2008, p. 284

16 Crookall, Robert, *The Supreme Adventure*, James Clarke & Co., Ltd., Cambridge, 1961, p. 46

17 Swedenborg, Emanuel, *Heaven & Hell*, Swedenborg Foundation, West Chester, PA, 1976, p. 364

18 Davis, Andrew Jackson, *Death and the After Life*, Colby & Rich, Banner Publishing House, Boston, 1865, p.21

19 Swain, Jasper, *On the Death of my Son*, The Aquarian Press, Northhamptonshire, England, 1989, p. 23

20 Schulthorp, Frederick C., *Excursions to the Spirit World*, The Greater World Assoc., London, 1961, p. 92

6

MANY MANSIONS

*The principal difficulty confronting the survival
hypothesis is an intelligible Hereafter.*
— **H. H. Price,** Oxford professor of logic

A
s the last few ounces of life force drained from the hunched, weary bodies of my parents, I helplessly watched them struggle to overcome the fear, the anxiety, the depression, and the strife so often associated with dying. I could feel their inner turmoil, their heavy hearts, their imprisoned souls. I could see clouds of despair over them. I could sense them blindly groping in the bondage imposed on them by their religious indoctrination. Their obligatory attendance at Sunday Mass provided them no comfort, no enlightenment, no hope. I wanted so badly to share with them the hope, the freedom, the splendor, the harmony, the beauty, the happiness, and the love I had come to associate with the life that awaited them after death, but the fetters that bound them to the walls of superstition were much too strong.

That superstition includes a horrific hell, a humdrum heaven, and in between, a painful purgatory in which souls must spend time – probably years, possibly decades, perhaps even centuries – purging their sins. It is in purgatory where my parents expected to reside when they transitioned; however, their belief that purgatory is preferable to hell offered them little solace. The Catholic Church had indoctrinated them with the idea that this in-between state is just as terrible as hell, the "flames" just as searing, the anguish just as great. The only difference is that they will someday be able to escape that inferno for heaven, where they might then aimlessly float around on clouds. Only a saintly few supposedly stand any chance of avoiding purgatory and going directly to heaven.

How can anyone anticipating such torment not approach death with great dread? Is it any wonder that so many people consider the loss of earthly consciousness as a morbid, chaotic, and depressing event and live their final years in a morass of doubt and fear? Why can't the Church see what a cruel, capricious, vindictive, and wrathful God it offers? Why doesn't the Church grasp the reason so many thinking people have abandoned it?

Apparently, some liberal thinkers in the Church have backed off the hell-like environment of purgatory, but they still see it as a place of suffering. Whatever the views of the Church liberals these days, it has not been effectively communicated to the faithful. After two-thousand years, the Church continues to use fear as a weapon to maintain its flock.

As mentioned in the Introduction, Martin Luther certainly didn't care much for purgatory. It was the primary issue giving rise to his break with the Catholic Church. Luther rebelled against the corruption involved with buying indulgences to shorten one's sentence in purgatory. Rather than attempt to make sense of purgatory, Protestantism has offered us a black and white afterlife, a dichotomy that is even more difficult to swallow than the Catholic view. Good and evil are absolutes.

Had my parents been Protestants, they might not have feared death quite as much as they did, but I doubt that the prospect of "sleeping" until Judgment Day or spending all of their time singing hymns and praising God in some staging area for Heaven would have significantly affected their outlook. Had they been non-believers, a march toward extinction might have been preferable to burning in purgatory, as another relative reasoned, but few people can get excited about "nothingness."

All major religions teach that in some manner human consciousness survives bodily death and sooner or later is awakened in a non-material environment. Nirvana, Gan Eden, Heaven, Paradise, Sheol, Purgatory, Hades, Gehenna, and Hell are some of the names assigned to afterlife destinations. These environments range from indescribable and incomprehensible bliss to unspeakable and unimaginable torment. Seemingly, a life of love and service should result in the blissful state, but some major belief systems hold that even a life devoted to love and service is not enough to warrant the blissful environment in the "after-life" if the individual has not bowed to the proper Savior or God or has not fully subscribed to the peculiar dictates of its particular dogma and doctrine. The predominant religious thinking seems to be that we end our earthly lives being labeled either "righteous" or "wicked" – no in-between – and our new environment is either positive or negative.

In the blissful state, we should find, according to some religions, souls who led selfish and hateful lives but who repented on their deathbeds or "found" their Savior just before dying and suddenly became righteous. Among the tormented, we should expect to find souls who led righteous lives for most of their years but who transgressed just before dying or never recognized their Savior.

It is difficult to reconcile much of what major religions consider the proper station in the afterlife with the loving, forgiving, and just God they see as governing that afterlife.

In John 14:2, Jesus says, "In my Father's house are many mansions. If it were not so I would have told you." Greek scholars tell us the Greek word translated to mansions originally meant a stopping place or a temporary abode. The usual orthodox Christian interpretation of that is that Jesus was referring only to Heaven. However, modern revelation suggests that Jesus was referring to the whole spectrum of the afterlife, from what is termed Hell on "up" through different realms or planes or spheres until we reach Heaven. This is somewhat consistent with the Buddhist view holding many states until reaching Nirvana or true Heaven and it is the primary lesson coming to us through Spiritual-ism. These states are also referred to as spheres, planes, realms, dimen-sions, and levels of vibration. They involve moving from darkness in the lower spheres to overwhelming brightness on the higher ones. The third sphere or plane, referred to by Spiritualists as "Summerland," is said to be where the average decent soul finds him- or herself imme-diately after death. The conditions there are said to be much the same as on the earth plane.

Emanuel Swedenborg* wrote that he discovered infinite diversi-ty in "heaven" and "countless communities" during his clairvoyant explorations. Like Swedenborg, Edgar Cayce, the famous American "sleeping prophet" of the last century, also told of taking a tour of many realms during one of his out-of-body experiences. He described how he encountered a stream of light he knew he must follow. In the lower or darker realms he saw "forms" that were floundering or lost and seeking the light. As the light grew stronger and stronger, he arrived at a place where individuals appeared much as they do today. Some seemed content, while others were striving for greater knowledge and light.

As discussed in Chapter I, Dr. George T. Dexter, a New York physician, reluctantly became a medium and began receiving many profound messages from Swedenborg and Sir Francis Bacon. On May 22, 1853, Swedenborg communicated that the moral condition of the spirits of the lower spheres does not appear to differ materially from the moral condition of the unprogressive man in our world. "They may, it is true, have moments when their spirits yearn for the brighter spheres beyond their dark plane, when conscious of its birthright, the soul awakens to a sense of its own degradation, and realizes its true situation," he wrote through Dexter's hand, "but they live and act as unprogressive man does, daily performing their accustomed round of malicious action, and carrying out the designs of their blunted perceptions; and it is not till some event, out of the ordinary occurrences of life, arouses them completely and opens their understanding to the reception of truth, that they begin to progress. There is so little difference in the whole action of spirit-life from your life, except that one step forward has been made – I do not refer to the higher spheres, of course – that the correspondence is almost exact." [1]

Swedenborg went on to say that spirits in the lower spheres live as if they do not realize there is anything beyond their own misty dwelling places, and as if they are incapable of being impressed with good and true.

On September 25, 1853, one of the circle sitters, a Mr. Warren, asked Bacon what impelled spirits in the lower and darker spheres to choose to go there and remain there indefinitely. "The reason is obvious," Bacon replied. "The great law of like attracting like obtains throughout the whole of the spheres. When a departed spirit enters into the spheres, he is at once attracted where he finds congeniality of place and persons. They could not be happy in the bright spheres. They could find no enjoyment where there is either virtue or goodness. Thus their first efforts are to locate themselves where the acquired attributes of mind in all its workings may be gratified. Their bodies are gross and their minds still grosser." [2]

Bacon added that there is in this condition of both body and mind a state which rejects magnetically all above and they are compelled to take a place appropriate for their moral advancement or lack thereof.

He said that the law of affinity is manifest as much in the higher spheres as in the lower, and that no spirit can become bad all at once or good instantly, adding that the law of progression and retrogression is in full force in all spheres.

Within two or three years of the communications coming through Dr. Dexter, Professor Robert Hare received similar messages. As he came to understand the afterlife environment, there are many graduations between the lowest degrees of vice, ignorance, and folly and the highest degrees of virtue, learning, and wisdom. When we cross over to the other side after physical death, we take our place based on what Hare called a "moral specific gravity," as discussed in Chapter V.

A renowned inventor and professor emeritus of chemistry in the University of Pennsylvania, Hare initially denounced the "popular madness" called Spiritualism by the American press and was intent on debunking it. However, Hare was astounded when he sat with several mediums and was provided with personal information, purportedly coming from spirits, which he was certain the medium could not have known or researched. Still, he remained skeptical. "In common with almost all educated persons of the nineteenth century, I had been brought up deaf to any testimony which claimed assistance from supernatural causes, such as ghosts, magic, or witchcraft," Hare explained his stubbornness.[3] But the evidence was too great and Hare was won over to a belief in Spiritualism.

Inventor that he was, Hare immediately went to work contriving an apparatus which would facilitate and expedite communication, as the process he had observed was very slow. He devised a machine, called a spiritoscope, with a circular disc, the letters of the alphabet around the circumference of the disc, and with weights, pulleys, and cords attaching it to the tilting table. The medium would sit behind the table in order to supply the "psychic force" through which the spirits caused the table to tilt, but the medium could not see the wheel and had no idea what was being spelled out.

Put to the test, the contraption worked and the first spirit to communicate was Hare's deceased father, Robert Sr., who had been a prominent Philadelphia merchant and politician, rising to the position of Speaker of the Senate of the State of Pennsylvania. When Hare continued to doubt, his father came through again and told him to listen to reason.

According to the senior Hare, the phenomena of Spiritualism was "a deliberate effort on the part of the inhabitants of the higher spheres to break through the partition which has interfered with the attainment, by mortals, of a correct idea of their destiny after death." He further explained to his son that a delegation of advanced spirits had been appointed for the project, the ultimate goal being to replace blind faith with a positive philosophy.

Mentioning a case where there was mischievous displacement of furniture by the spirits, Hare asked his father why low spirits were allowed to interfere in the undertaking. His father explained that the spirits in the lower spheres are better able to make mechanical movements and loud rappings, and their assistance was required. He further said that the raps were produced by voluntary discharges of the vitalized spiritual electricity emanating from the medium. The spirits can direct these discharges at will to any particular locality, thereby producing sounds or concussion. It was further explained that things such as levitation of tables, which did not involve communication, were simply to get attention and create interest.

As soon as he was convinced that the phenomena were credible reports from spirits of the dead, Hare began asking about their abodes, their modes of existence, their theological doctrines, and diversities of their situations. He was told that there are seven spheres, the terrestrial sphere occupied by humans being the first, while the second sphere is where depraved spirits find themselves until they can begin the process of purification that allows them to ascend to higher spheres. When spirits reach the seventh sphere, they are entitled to enter the supernal heaven. He was also informed that there are no visible boundaries between spheres, but spirits have a peculiar sense which makes them understand when they are passing from one sphere to another.

"The most favorable idea of heaven given in Scripture seems to be that which identifies it with Paradise," Hare wrote. "In other words, a most beautiful garden. But who would conceive an *eternal* residence in one garden, however superlative its attractions, as desirable? The idea of the spheres assumes a succession of gardens, with every pleasure, every joy of which the human heart and intellect are capable; and beyond those gardens the whole universe is open to us, and an ultimate ministration as angels under our Heavenly Father." [4]

Hare's discarnate father further explained that the spirit goes to a sphere for which it is morally and intellectually adapted; thus, the first sphere above the terrestrial one, i.e., the second sphere, is the abode of "degraded" spirits, meaning not only evil spirits but "misdirected" ones as well. He pointed out that there are millions of such spirits in the second sphere, what religions call Hell, Hades, or Purgatory, who are groping and unable to free themselves from the fetters of earthly conditions. This sphere is said to be the abode of as many spirits as all the five spheres above it. Nevertheless, contrary to the teachings of many religions, the spirits on this sphere are not permanently confined there as "onward and upward" is the motto of the spirit world. Sooner or later, spirits from higher levels are able to reach them and help them see the light.

Because of the barriers spirits must overcome in communicating with the material world, the senior Hare warned his son to discern the messages and not take everything literally: "As there are no words in the human language in which spiritual ideas may be embodied so as to convey their literal and exact signification, we are obliged ofttimes to have recourse to the use of analogisms and metaphorical modes of expression. In our communion with you we have to comply with the peculiar structure and rules of your language; but the genius of our language is such that we can impart more ideas to each other in a single word than you can possibly convey in a hundred."[5]

Hare informed his son that the spheres revolve with the earth on a common axis around the sun, but they are not dependent on the sun for either light or heat. Rather, the spirit receives light and heat from his internal or spiritual correspondence. He said that they have no division of time. "Although we, like you, are constantly progressing toward perfection, our ideas of time and the seasons differ widely from yours; with you it is time – with us, eternity," he continued. "In the terrestrial sphere, a man's thoughts, being bounded by time and space, are limited; but with us they are extended in proportion as we get rid of those restrictions and our perceptions of truth become more accurate."[6]

Each sphere, the senior Hare said, is divided into six circles, or societies, in which congenial spirits are united and subsist together according to the law of affinity. While these spirits generally agree in moral and intellectual matters, there are individual differences and some disagreements. Spirits united by ties of consanguinity and marriage may or may not be linked together in the spheres and in the same society. It depends on the affinity between them, including the level of advancement. However, a spirit in a higher sphere can pass to a lower one to visit with loved ones. But a spirit can never ascend to the higher spheres until fully prepared for such a transition.

Each society has teachers from those above, as well as from higher spheres, whose duty it is to impart knowledge acquired from their instructions and experience. "Thus, by receiving and giving knowledge our moral and intellectual faculties are expanded to higher conceptions and more exalted views of the great Creator, whose almighty power is no less displayed in the constitution of spirit worlds, than in that of the countless resplendent orbs of space."[7]

But they do more than study. It was explained that they have many sources of intellectual, moral, and heartfelt enjoyment from which they derive ineffable pleasures, one of which is social reunions and convivial meetings – a coming together of friends, brothers, sisters, children, and parents, where the tenderest affections are excited and the fondest and most endearing reminiscences are awakened, where spirit meets in unison with spirit.

A spirit named Maria, the daughter of Professor Hare's friend, communicated with her father through the mediumship of Mrs. M. B. Gourlay while Hare observed and recorded. She told her father that when she awakened in the spirit world she felt as if she were coming out of a deep sleep and that it was some time before she could collect her scattered senses. She recalled that the racking pains she had felt before giving up the ghost had all fled and she felt a newness of life. She saw indistinct and shadowy forms flitting before her and soon realized that they were her departed friends. Her first concern was for those grieving her death. As her vision became clearer, she perceived a group from which her brother William emerged to greet her. He accompanied her to the third sphere, but they had to pass through the second sphere. She described it as gloomy and uncomfortable, appearing like a vast desert without a green spot to relieve the eyes. She observed its denizens straggling here and there with no fixed objective in view. "All are seeking to minister to their perverted tastes. Some are holding forth in loud tones, and painting in false and gaudy colors the joy of their home," Maria communicated. "Others, who occupied high stations on earth, hang their heads in confusion, and would fain hide themselves from view; but they are taunted with rude jests, and told that their 'pride of position will avail them nothing here.' One heart-sickening feature of this place is the absence of children. No purity can exist where such evils abound. 'The loud laugh, which bespeaks the vacant mind' is heard pealing forth in derision, as the teachers from the higher spheres approach the motley group. Some, in whom the work of regeneration has commenced, are seen ascending the spiral stairway of progress which leads to the third sphere."[8]

On approaching the third sphere, Maria and William were met by a company of angels from the seventh sphere, among whom she recognized two brothers who had died in infancy and had since grown to the stature of men. She said that the law of affinity drew her toward them. They welcomed her and informed her that another link was added to the chain of love which bound them together. Maria informed her father that the beauty of the third sphere far transcends that of earth. She described the scenery as endlessly diversified with spiritual objects corresponding to things on the earth plane. "Mountains and valleys, hills and dales, rivers and lakes, and trees and plants lend their enchantment to the scene," she related. "The inhabitants of this sphere are anxious for instruction. The teachers from the higher degrees are listened to with profound respect and attention."[9]

Maria witnessed a group enter a large temple, where a teacher was waiting to address them. She described the temple as immensely large and symmetrical in its proportions. The material appeared similar in appearance to alabaster but was transparent. The seats were semicircular forming an amphitheater. The speaker talked about the "light that is within you." But Maria's new home was not in the third sphere. They were just passing through en route to her home in the fourth sphere, where she found still more beautiful landscapes, a greener green, and flowers more gorgeous in their hue. "All have an interior language which spirits alone can fully comprehend," she continued...."Here, too, are sparkling streams, murmuring cascades and gushing fountains, and trees bending beneath their load of golden fruit; and here are temples devoted to the arts and sciences."[10]

Maria went on to describe a building devoted to the teachers from the seventh sphere with multitudes thronging in its portals. She observed a band of children carrying wreaths of flowers and singing after welcoming a child just escaped from the earth plane. And while she had never been to the fifth, sixth, or seventh spheres, she had been told about them. Each one was more magnificent than the sphere below it. The fifth sphere, she was informed, has lovely villas, beautiful temples, forest-crowned hills, and gently undulating plains. She said that she could not begin to describe the sixth and seventh spheres as her vocabulary was too limited to give a just conception of them. Among the residents of the seventh sphere, she had been informed, were Jesus of Nazareth, John the beloved, Confucius, Seneca, Plato, Socrates, and Solon.

Hare's deceased sister, Martha, also communicated, telling him that the language of mortals is inadequate to convey even a tenth part of the joy that she experienced when liberated from the physical body.

She recalled being dazzled by brilliant light emanated by the beings who surrounded her, as she passed from death to life, and welcomed her. Their father was the first to greet her. "Father watched my emotion with deep interest, and was delighted with the startling and happy effect produced on my mind," she communicated. "We passed quickly through the different stages of our progress, till we arrived at the fifth spiritual sphere, which is my present home. I am often with my friends on earth, and would gladly influence them, and prove my identity to them, if they would render themselves receptive to my power...When we desire to be with our friends on earth, we have only to will it, and our desire is instantly gratified. We can visit the spheres below, but not those above us until we are prepared for admission into them by a gradual process of development." [11]

Martha reiterated much of what her brother had heard from their father and from Maria. She also mentioned that the second sphere, or first spiritual sphere, is the abode of those spirits whose desires are low and sensuous. They maintain interests in the things that attracted them on earth until their moral faculties become strengthened. Each individual in the spirit world, she explained, is judged and suffers according to the deeds done in the body. But Martha was quick to inform her brother that she could not tell him everything about the spheres. "It is thought by many of our brothers in the flesh that we will impart to them all the knowledge that we possess respecting the mysteries of the spheres," she further communicated, "but on this point let them be undeceived, for it is utterly impossible for them to comprehend all in their present rudimental state. Our chief objective is to assure them, by unmistakable signs, of the soul's immortality, and the conditions necessary to be observed by them in order to obtain a happy future existence." [12]

Hare's son, Theodore, who died in 1825, when he was only five months old, also communicated. He informed his father that he had no recollection of his earth-life, but that he had learned all about it as he developed in the spirit world. When Hare asked Theodore how he came to understand the material world, Theodore replied that he had frequently visited earth and had often accompanied his father in his daily walks and study and had continued to learn from him and his mother during his early years in spirit.

When Hare gave a talk to the American Association for the Advancement of Science, discussing his spirit research, some members of the organization called for his expulsion from the organization. However, this apparently resulted in Hare becoming even more entrenched in his belief and he went to his grave certain that there was something beyond death. "No evidence of any important truth in science" he offered, "can be shown to be more unexceptionable than that which I have received of this glorious fact that heaven is really 'at hand,' and that our relatives, friends, and acquaintances who are worthy of happiness while describing themselves as ineffably happy, are still progressing to higher felicity; and while hovering aloft in our midst, are taking interest in our welfare with an augmented zeal or affection, so that, by these means, they may be a solace to us, in despite of death." [13]

When Anglican priest William Stainton Moses*, also a reluctant medium, asked the apparently advanced spirit known as Imperator about the spheres, Imperator explained that they are states, not places, as Moses understood them. The difference between spheres, he said, is based upon the moral, intellectual, and spiritual state of the inhabitants. Imperator went on to say that the progress of spirits is made through seven states, during which the spirit is laboring either to purge away the contracted impurities of earth or to gain further knowledge to prepare oneself for a life of contemplation. "The first three spheres are near about your earth," Imperator communicated. "They are filled thus. The first with those who, from many causes, are attracted to earth. Such are they who have made little progress in the earth sphere; not the wholly bad, but the vacillating, aimless souls who have frittered away their opportunities and made no use of them. Those, again, whom the affections and affinity for pursuits of their friends restrain them from soaring, and who prefer to remain near the earth sphere, though they might progress. In addition, there are the imperfectly trained souls whose education is still young, and who are in course of elementary training; those who have been incarnated in imperfect bodies, and have to learn still what they should have learned on earth. Those, too, who have been prematurely withdrawn from earth, and from no fault of their own, have still to learn before they can progress." [14]

A discarnate friend, identified as Bishop Samuel Wilberforce when on earth, told Moses that they have gatherings and are banded together under the government of wiser and higher spirits, much like government on earth. Disobedience of the laws is punished by a course of instruction, while repeated errors causes removal to a lower plane until experience has fitted the spirit to rise. Imperator broke in and told Moses that his friend was referring only to what he has seen in the lower spheres, and said that they were states of probation and preparation.

Moses asked about reincarnation and was told that only the most advanced Intelligences are able to discourse on that subject and that it is not given to the lower ranks of the spiritual hierarchy to know. It was unclear as to whether one was to infer from this that Imperator and his band were not high enough to explain reincarnation, but Imperator said that reincarnation is not true in the sense in which it is popularly understood. He added: "There are still mysteries, we are fain to confess, into which it is not well that man should penetrate. One of such mysteries is the ultimate development and destiny of spirits. Whether in the eternal counsels of the Supreme it may be deemed well that a particular spirit should or should not be again incarnated in a material form is a question than none can answer, for none can know, not even the spirit's own guides. What is wise and well will be done...There are other aspects of the question which, in the exercise of our discretion, we withhold; the time is not yet come for them. Spirits cannot be expected to know all abstruse mysteries, and those who profess to do so give the best proof of their falsity." [15] (See Appendix B for more on reincarnation)

A Wesleyan minister, Charles Drayton Thomas was one of the lead investigators for the Society for Psychical Research (SPR) in the study of the mediumship of Gladys Osborne Leonard, with whom he had more than 500 sittings, beginning in 1917. He received many messages from his father, who had passed over in 1903, and from his sister. After initially focusing on the evidential, Thomas began asking his father about some aspects of the afterlife, including what he saw above him. The discarnate father described it as "atmosphere," looking much like our sky but without clouds. To pass from one sphere to another, he said that there are channels or clearings, much like tunnels, which have been bored mentally. When Drayton asked his father about the governing forces involved in the various spheres or planes, his father answered: "When one is fitted only for a low plane, no amount of desire to be on a higher or more beautiful one would suffice to take one there. The habit of life on earth decides, and not any chance desire. If a man has qualified for a lower sphere, he will find himself there and he cannot get away from it. That is just and right, and it saves a vast amount of supervision. According as the soul moulds itself while in the body, so it decides the place to which it must go on leaving the body. Those who simply live in the physical senses find themselves exceedingly limited on leaving earth. We wish such people understood the facts, so that they might realize how fatally unwise and short-sighted is their manner of life." [16]

The senior Thomas, who said he was on the third sphere, explained that the lower the sphere, the more correspondence there is with places on earth. One can even find slums and other undesirable features of earth cities. As one advances to higher spheres, there is less and less resemblance to earth conditions. Although he had not been to those higher spheres, teachers from higher spheres had so informed him. Moreover, as one advances toward the seventh sphere, he will find more perfect operation of divine law or principle. He added that there are trees, grass, and flowers in his sphere as well as other forms which he could not describe because they were beyond his son's conception and language.

Etta, Thomas's sister, communicated that spirits on the lower spheres are unable to see or grasp the divine plan and those on earth are also unable to understand it. "If the whole plan were given to you at once, you would probably be dazzled, confused, weighed down by it," Etta explained. "On those high spheres it is difficult for them to explain to me how they know things, because they can comprehend the whole, and although they are no longer in close touch with detail, yet detail is attended by them; for they do perfectly what they undertake." [17]

Etta likened it to asking an experienced pianist which notes his fingers are touching each moment. Since he sees the music more as a whole, he does not concern himself with which fingers are touching particular keys of the piano at a certain time. Thus, Etta explained, a beginning pianist might be better able to explain the elementary details and that is why most of the communication comes from the lower or intermediate spheres.

"Looking very far ahead indeed, I know there is a great destiny which awaits us some day, somewhere, somehow," the senior Thomas told his son. "We shall continue to be ourselves, but in a state higher than anything realized upon these spheres. I know that there is a world above and beyond our present one, but I do not seek to know too much until it is given to me." [18]

Alvin Mattson, a Lutheran minister who made his transition to the spirit world in 1970, is said to have communicated with his daughter, Ruth Mattson Taylor, through the British medium Margaret Flavell Tweddell. He, too, reported various planes of existence. "From this point we can progress to higher planes – to higher levels of consciousness," Mattson is quoted. "By 'higher' planes I do not mean spatially higher but rather those planes which have a finer vibration." Mattson went on to say that many of the religious denominations continue to

practice the rites of their respective churches on the lower or intermediate planes, where he made his abode, but that he had been permit-
ted to visit higher planes "where there is a unity of God-praise, not a
segregation of the praise of God." [19]

A century earlier, Andrew Jackson Davis reported that many souls
continue to subscribe to the same religious beliefs they held in the
physical world. He referred to this sphere, or section of the sphere, as
Altolissa. "Jews still believe in the doctrine of their fathers – Abraham,
Isaac, and Jacob; the Roman Catholics hold the same views they did
before death; and there are other sects in Altolissa who think and believe in the same things and forms of faith they learned on earth," he
stated, adding that they are so far below the 'higher planes' that this is
required in order to make them feel 'at home.' However, all eventually
evolve toward a single understanding of spirit.[20]

Almost without exception, we are told of progressive spheres, realms
or planes by various communicators. It is often reported that there are
seven basic planes, giving some credence to "Seventh Heaven" mythology, but many of the spirits communicating claim they do not know
how many planes there are because they know only of the plane on
which they live, those below, and perhaps, as with Mattson, those immediately above. Like Mattson and Thomas, many communicators have
reported that they have been able to visit higher planes for a short period, but that the light there is too great for them and they are forced
to return to their proper abode.

"These worlds above us are even richer in light and happiness," Mike
Swain communicated to his father, Jasper Swain, after Mike was killed
in a head-on collision. "If I go up there, and I can, I find it too bright;
the light hurts my eyes. And the vibrations are so refined that I can't
respond to them! So I reverse gear and return to *this* world – which
suits me just fine."

Mike Swain went on to say that the planes below him are denser and
dimmer. "If I go down to them, it becomes murkier and murkier until
it is so creepy that I scoot back here where I belong." [21]

"It is like knowledge," said Silver Birch, a spirit entity who spoke
through the British trance medium Maurice Barbanell* for some 50
years, ending around 1980. "The more you have, the more you realize there is further knowledge to be gained. The sphere or plane on
which you exist in our world contains individuals at the same state of
spiritual development as you are. You can't go spiritually higher until
you are ready. You can go lower, as many of us do in order to perform

missionary work among the unenlightened beings in the lower spheres. Progress consists of shedding imperfections and striving and growing toward perfection at all times."[22]

Reaching the highest sphere is sometimes referred to as "merging with the whole" or achieving "Oneness" with the Creator. This is not particularly appealing to some people as it suggests that we give up our individuality. Silver Birch said that such is not the case. "The ultimate is not the attainment of Nirvana," he communicated. "All spiritual progress is toward increasing individuality. You do not become less of an individual. You become more of an individual. You develop latent gifts, you acquire greater knowledge, your character becomes stronger, more of the divine is exhibited through you...You do not lose yourself. What you succeed in doing is finding yourself."[23]

Philip Gilbert, a sailor killed during World War II, communicated extensively with his mother, Alice Gilbert, by means of automatic writing. "The more I learn and merge into my true self, the more difficult it is to express what I see and do," he told her. "The only absolute certainty is that I, the central I, is unchanged and somewhat as you knew me, only more so. But my form dissolves and reforms itself at will now, for I can think myself into any semblance I please, to do my work."[24]

Frederic Myers communicated much the same message. "The merging with the Idea, with the Great Source of spirit, does not imply annihilation," he said. "You still exist as an individual. You are as a wave in the sea; and you at last entered into Reality and cast from you all illusions of appearances. But some intangible essence has been added to your spirit through its long habitation of matter, of ether the ancestor of matter, of what the scientists call empty space, though, if they but knew it, empty space is peopled with forms of an infinite fineness and variety."[25]

[1] Edmonds, John & Dexter, George T., *Spiritualism*, Partridge & Brittan, New York, 1853, p. 230

[2] _____ p. 203

[3] Hare, Robert, M.D., *Experimental Investigation of the Spirit Manifestations*, Partridge & Brittan, New York, 1855, p. 38

[4] _____ p. 142

[5] _____ p 96

[6] _____ p. 88

[7] _____ p. 89

[8] _____ p. 105

[9] _____ p. 106

[10] _____ p. 107

[11] _____ p. 110

[12] _____ p. 111

[13] _____ p. 428

[14] Moses, William Stainton, *More Spirit Teachings*, Meilach.com, Sec. II, p. 8

[15] _____ Sec. II, p. 6

[16] _____ Thomas, Charles Drayton, *Life Beyond Death with Evidence*, W. Collins Sons. & Co., Glasgow, 1928, p. 168

[17] _____ p. 170

[18] _____ p. 217

[19] Taylor, Ruth Mattson, *Witness from Beyond*, Hawthorn Books, Inc., New York, 1975, p. 43.

[20] Davis, Andrew Jackson, *Death and the After Life*, Colby & Rich, Boston, 1865, p. 95

[21] Swain, Jasper, *On the Death of My Son*, The Aquarian Press, UK, 1989, p. 24

[22] Ballard, Stan A. & Green, Roger, *The Silver Birch Book of Questions & Answers*, Spiritual Truth Press, London, 1998, p. 39

[23] _____ p. 162

[24] Gilbert, Alice, *Philip in the Spheres*, The Aquarian Press, London, 1952, p. 93

[25] Cummins, Geraldine, *The Road to Immortality*, The Aquarian Press, London, 1955, p. 72

7

MAKING SENSE OF THE AFTERLIFE

Even those of us who consider there may be a next world are likely to conceive of it as some spiritual dimension quite unlike the hard physicality of this world. The idea that there may be not only landscapes similar to ours but even houses and cities takes us way past the threshold of disbelief.
— **David Fontana,** Ph.D.

Although I find very little on television that interests me these days, I admit to having been hooked on the "24" action series before it ended a year or two ago. I would get so into the excitement at times that I found myself on the edge of my seat and "living" the action. When a segment of the series would end on its usual cliffhanger with a commercial following, I would be reminded it is just TV fiction, not real life. But my consciousness would not fully accept the fiction or unreality of it. Some part of my consciousness still held on to the emotion and action of it while anxiously awaiting the next segment to see what would happen to Jack Bauer, the hero of the series.

When a trip prevented me from seeing a weekly segment of "24" during its final year, I felt conflicted. I *had* to know what happened. My mind tried to reason with my consciousness by re-"minding" it that it isn't real and that I shouldn't care what happened, but my consciousness struggled to accept what the mind was telling it and I was determined to see the next segment.

On the other hand, I don't lose myself in movies as much as many people do. My wife refuses to watch bloody scenes and if one catches her by surprise she will let out a scream. I have no difficulty watching such scenes, although I'm sure that if I were witnessing them in real life my reaction would be much different. Thus, even though I am somewhat absorbed in the movie and not completely distinguishing between reality and unreality, my consciousness is straddling the "threshold of awareness" enough so that I do not react too emotionally to violent scenes.

Similar difficulties in distinguishing between the *real* and the unreal apparently take place in the afterlife, at least during the early stages. We are told by credible spirit communicators that it takes longer for the spiritually-challenged soul to make the distinction than it does for the spiritually developed, and that it is a matter of degree of the development of consciousness. Consider, for example, reports through mediums that spirits continue to wear clothes, live in houses, eat, drink, and perhaps even play golf. Such reports are enough to discredit the whole idea of an afterlife. "How absolutely ridiculous!" is the typical reaction of the skeptic and debunker, who find much humor in it all. But to the discerning person, it may not be as ridiculous as it sounds.

After Mike Swain died in a head-on collision, he informed his father that when he first arrived in his new environment the routines of eating, drinking, and sleeping were too firmly established to be eliminated all at once. "So if you think you need to sleep, well you lay down on a couch in one of the houses, and you sleep for as long as you want. If you think you need to eat, then you eat your fill. There are no excretory organs in our bodies. For example, when I drink a glass of water, it just diffuses itself throughout my system, and that's that! In other words, it's converted into energy. If I see a beautiful apple tree with bright red apples on it, I can reach up and pick one off and swallow it – all it does is to give me a tingling sense of satisfaction."

When Mike's father asked him about clothing, Mike replied that it was just a matter of concentrating on a particular cut of clothes and he would be wearing it. When they had public gatherings or when a teacher from higher spheres came down to lecture in the halls of wisdom, he would discard his personal preference and wear his spirit robe. These robes come in a spectrum of glowing colors, which reflect the true condition of the individual spirit. "Most of us here wear our spirit clothing most of the time," he said. "When we combine this with our gift of telepathy, it's well nigh impossible for anyone to maintain a phony front and hope to get away with it. No sooner have I *thought* a think, than the person I'm talking to *hears* it. He knows exactly what's making me tick."[1]

When Frederick C. Sculthorp took a tour of the lower realms during one of his many out-of-body experiences, he witnessed a hut with long tables with rows of plates. Each plate had one slice of bread with a small portion of jam on it. "I was told that these people had been some time in spirit but were quite ignorant of the fact and the meager ration was an endeavor to wean them from desire for food," he recorded, adding that the lower spheres are quite earth-like and quite solid when the spirit body assumes the same wavelength.[2]

Silver Birch, the high spirit or group soul who spoke through the trance mediumship of Maurice Barbanell* for many years, said that the next stage of life is a replica of our world of matter. "Were it not so, the shock for the many who are uninstructed and ignorant would be more than they could stand," Silver Birth explained. "And so it has to be accomplished by very easy stages. The next stage of life resembles your world. That is why so many do not know that they have passed beyond the physical."[3]

Silver Birch added that it is a world of thought and that thought is reality. The "dream life" is a necessary part of adjusting and awakening. For those completely ignorant of the spirit world, there is a complete replica of everything, Silver Birch pointed out. Since spiritual consciousness is a matter of degree rather than stepping over some threshold into a world of enlightenment, even spiritually evolved souls may experience the "dream life" to some extent. "The higher your consciousness, the less the need for adjustment," Silver Birch stressed.[4]

On March 11, 1932, Raymond Lodge attempted to explain conditions on his side of the veil to his father, Sir Oliver Lodge*. "Father, we are obliged to create conditions, and what you might call things, on our plane," Raymond stated through the vocal cords of Gladys Osborne Leonard. "They've only got a temporary life. They are illusions, something to the same extent as a materialization is an illusion. On your side, you have something material for the time being. It's something natural in appearance, in feel, apparently in every way it appeals to the senses of *this* body (the entranced medium touching Sir Oliver). On our side we are bound to create certain things, houses, clothes, partially for the time being, in order to make a satisfactory harmonious and suitable setting for the soul to live in and work in. And they become a medium of expression...It's one of the necessary illusions of our life."

When Sir Oliver asked Raymond if he was saying that he lived in a world of illusion, Raymond replied that he was in an extension of the illusory world in which his father was living. "We are in touch with a world of reality because we are in the outer rim of the world of illusion," he explained to Sir Oliver. "We're more sure of the world of reality than you are. Father, the spirit universe is the world of reality. Spirit and mind both belong to the world of reality. Everything else, that is, external things, are in a sense necessary for a time, but superfluous and only temporary in existence as far as the world of reality goes – which is external and indestructible. Spirit and mind belong to that world...We are not entirely free from your world of matter, we are more independent of it, but are still concerned with it."

Sir Oliver pondered on the situation in writing: "I know that its inhabitants say it is extraordinarily like the earth, that they have flowers, and trees and houses, and can get anything they want by merely wishing for it, which seems rather strange, but I was not prepared to think of it as a world of illusion wherein all such objects of sense were illusory."

In further discussing the matter with Raymond and Frederic W. H. Myers*, his old friend and fellow psychical researcher who had died in 1901 and who also communicated through Mrs. Leonard, Sir Oliver concluded that it was a temporary environment for spirits who have recently crossed over and still making adjustments before going on to realms of higher vibration, which become less and less illusory and more and more real as a soul advances in the spirit world. "We are not transported to the full blaze of reality all at once," Lodge surmised, pointing out that a table that feels solid and substantial is really a multitude of whirling electrons with great spaces between them and that when we stand on the floor we are bombarded upwards and supported by a great multitude of little blows delivered by the atoms beneath our feet.[5] As none of this is apparent to the ordinary senses, it can be considered illusory, Sir Oliver concluded, even though we choose to interpret it in a way that appeals to our coarse-grained sense organs.

When Raymond Lodge first began communicating with his father and mother some 10 weeks after his death in 1915, the subject of clothing came up. "Can you fancy seeing me in white robes?" Raymond communicated to his mother. "Mind, I didn't care for them at first, and I wouldn't wear them. Just like a fellow gone to a country where there is a hot climate – an ignorant fellow, not knowing what he is going to; it's just like that. He may make up his mind to wear his own clothes a little while, but he will soon be dressing like the natives."

Raymond went on to tell his mother that he was allowed to have earth clothes until he got acclimated. "I don't think I will ever be able to make the boys see me in white robes," Raymond added, apparently jesting. [6]

As Myers explained it through the hand of Geraldine Cummins* a number of years after his communication with Sir Oliver, nearly every soul lives for a time in the state of illusion, thinking that substance is reality. "They are not prepared for an immediate and complete change of outlook," Myers said. "They passionately yearn for familiar though idealized surroundings. Their will to live is merely to live, therefore, in the past. So they enter that dream I call Illusion-land."

Myers pointed out that the average unthinking man in the street may desire a glorified brick villa and will likely find it. If he were to long for a superior brand of cigar, he can have the experience of smoking this brand. If he wanted to play golf, he may continue to play golf. "But he is merely dreaming all the time or, rather, living within the fantasy created by his strongest desires on earth. After a while this life of pleasure ceases to amuse and content him. Then he begins to think and long for the unknown, long for a new life. He is at last prepared to make the leap in evolution and this cloudy dream vanishes." [7]

Long before Raymond Lodge and Frederic W. H. Myers reported on the afterlife environment, Emanuel Swedenborg* said that angels live together as people on earth do and "they have clothes, houses, and many similar things." [8] He explained that clothes correspond to their advancement in the spirit world. The more advanced have clothes that gleam as if aflame, some radiant as if alight. The less advanced have shining white clothes without radiance, while those even lower in advancement have clothes of various colors.

"When the soul leaves the body it is at the first moment quite unclothed as at birth," Julia Ames communicated to William T. Stead* after her physical death. "I awoke standing by my dead body, thinking I was still alive and in my ordinary physical frame," Julia penned through Stead's hand by means of automatic writing. "It was only when I saw the corpse in the bed that I knew that something had happened. When the thought of nakedness crosses the spirit there comes the clothing which you need. The idea with us is creative. We think, and the thing is. I do not remember putting on any garments. There is just the sense of need, and the need is supplied."

Julia added that once the spirit has fully awakened and adapted to the new environment, it has the ability to make itself appear in different ways, e.g., to appear as a child to someone who knew the spirit, when in the flesh, only as a child. "We have no need to do so for our own purposes, but when a newcomer arrives, or when we have to manifest ourselves to you who are still in the body, then we need to use this thought-creation, and body forth the visual tangible appearances with which you are familiar."[9]

After dying in the Titanic disaster of 1912, Stead began communicating through various mediums and appearing at some materialization séances. He explained that there were souls on his side who had the power of sensing people (mediums) who could be used for communication. One such soul helped him find mediums and showed him how to make his presence known. It was explained to him that he had to visualize himself among the people in the flesh and imagine that he was standing there in the flesh with a strong light thrown upon himself. "Hold the visualization very deliberately and in detail, and keep it fixed upon my mind, that at that moment I *was* there and they were conscious of it," Stead described the process.

Stead added that the people at one sitting were able to see only his face because he had visualized only his face. "I imagined the part they would recognize me by."[10] It was in the same way he was able to get a message through. He stood by the medium, concentrated his mind on a short sentence, and repeated it with much emphasis and deliberation until he could hear part of it spoken through the medium.

A sitter at one of the séances of D. D. Home, the renowned medium of yesteryear, asked Home's spirit control how spirits make themselves visible. "At times we make passes (augment the field of energy) over the individual to cause him to see us; sometimes we make the actual resemblance of our former clothing appear exactly as we were known to you on earth," came the reply. "Sometimes we project an image that you see; sometimes you see us as we are with a cloudlike aura of light around us."[11]

Other spirits who have materialized at séances or appeared in spirit photographs wear robes or earthly-type clothing, having to project an image of themselves into a fluid called ectoplasm. However, quite a few spirits do not appear exactly as their loved ones remember them. It seems that many spirits have only a vague recollection of their earthly appearance. One spirit communicating with Dr. Charles Richet, the 1913 Nobel Prize winner in medicine, told him that he could not materialize and show himself because he could not remember what he looked like when alive. It should be kept in mind that before photography many people had no real fixed image of what they looked like, nothing more than fleeting images from a faulty mirror or a pond. Moreover, many people now living may have a flattering self-image of themselves, perhaps an image that appears in a 20-year-old portrait sitting on the mantel.

Claude Kelway-Bamber, a British pilot killed during WWI, communicated with his mother through Gladys Osborne-Leonard*. "I dress as I did with you, but some people wear white robes because they think when out of the mortal body it is the correct thing to do," he told her. "If I chose to wear a tunic and sandals, or a 'Beefeater's' getup, no one would laugh and jeer; they would realize it made me happy, and that is reason enough."

Kelway-Bamber said that he was taken by his guides to a higher sphere to see Christ. "When the appointed time came, my guides provided me with a plain white robe to wear, and we passed through connecting shafts to the Christ-sphere. My general impression was that of brightness, almost dazzling; the air scintillated like diamonds – it almost crackled, it was so full of electricity; my feet had not a very firm grip of the ground." [12]

On September 12, 1945, Philip Gilbert, a sailor in the British navy killed in WWII, communicated with his mother, Alice Gilbert. "You want me to tell you more of conditions here," he communicated by means of automatic writing. "It's not easy to explain how one can be solid and yet not solid. Still, anyone who knows anything about physics and electrons knows that all earthly matter is just that – seeming solid and yet really a mass of vibrating particles. We are the same, I think, the body I use now looks to me very like my old one, but there are no organs, as you know. I think I function through my thought, somehow. I can will myself into any clothes I want. I usually get myself into my tweed coat and flannels...Some people go about seeing themselves in the most fantastic outfits. They are dressed as their inner nature builds them up. That is why, at first, Grandpa so often showed to mediums in a sort of black cassock, like a clergyman."

Philip added that people in higher planes become more and more luminous and that Christ is seen as a mass of violet golden light.

At a later sitting Philip told his mother that he had encountered a young woman who had been a model when alive and still did not realize she was "dead." "She still went parading up and down to an imaginary audience," he communicated. "But there were gleams in her of a capacity for service. When I spoke to her, she at first thought it was the prelude to adventure, so I had to do some little stunts to show her I was not an amorous sailor. In fact, I managed to wish myself into the garment of an Egyptian priest, for a moment, and then back again as the British navy once more – the poor thing thought she'd had one too many. However, little by little, I got her to understand that she had been killed by a 'V2' a year ago. At first she was rather upset, for she has little power of concentration, but soon, being quite a sensible wench, she got the idea and she perked up. Her first idea was to see herself in a few remarkable garments. She seems to have no relatives or friends here that I can find, but I think she has some intention of finding her family still on earth and parking herself near them for a time. You see how queer it all is, far different from the easy falling into heaven theories we were brought up on."

At still another sitting, Philip told his mother that he met a very attractive young woman, or, at least, she had been attractive when in her earthly shell. In fact, she had been obsessed with her beauty and was a very selfish woman. However, much of her beauty was due to heavy make-up. Like the model, the woman had yet to realize she was dead. "She had, of course, no idea how to create for herself, and she hovered miserably around the beauty parlours [on earth in an effort to tidy herself up.]" [13]

The Rev. G. Vale Owen, a clergyman of the Church of England, was also an automatic writer and received many messages from the spirit world, including from his deceased mother, who told him that the texture and hue of their garments take their quality from the spiritual state and character of the wearer. "The atmosphere also has an effect on our clothing, and enters into the influence of our own personalities in its effect on texture and colour," she communicated. "So that while, if we were all of the same quality spiritually our clothing would be of the same tint and texture, by reason of the atmospheric influence, this is in fact modified by the degree in which our own characters differ one from another...Also the tint of our robes changes according to the part of the grounds in which we happen to be. It is very interesting and instructive, and also very beautiful, to see them change as one turns down a side walk where different vegetation flourishes, or where the arrangement of the various species of plants is different." [14]

Gordon Burdick told medium Grace Rosher that reality on his side was much like what he had experienced when alive in the flesh. "Life here is in a sense a continuation of our existence on earth, and not of an unfamiliar kind," he wrote. "We have work to do. It is not just one long holiday. We live under conditions much like those on earth. We have homes, there are places of entertainment and of learning. The children are brought up in very much the same way as in the old world." [15]

Communicating through the hand of Wellesley Tudor Pole, Thomas Dowding, who died during World War I at age 37, said that he didn't want to believe that what he was now experiencing in his *present life*, were mere illusions, just as his earth life was nothing more than an illusion. "Unfortunately, I fear it may be true," he continued. "I have given the matter much thought. Evidently I am in a state of conscious-ness not far removed from earthly existence. I am journeying toward a wider, truer life, but I am not yet there…Anyway, my life seems quite as real as it did on earth, even more real. There is *something* that lives and moves within me that is *not* illusion. That something will forge its way out into the light some day." [16]

In communicating with his mother, Wadsworth Cecil Tuck, who claimed to be on the third sphere, said that he sometimes sees an old friend and cannot always tell if the friend is actually there. "Even when I meet friends in the third sphere, I cannot tell whether they are over here by dream or by real," he said. "The dream things are very like the real things, unless, as I say, one has studied chemistry, and can sepa-rate." [17]

When William Stainton Moses* asked if homes in the spirit world are material, Imperator replied in the affirmative but added that they are not material in the sense that Moses counts matter. He cautioned Moses not to accept everything literally as so much of what he had to say had no counterpart in the material world. Thus, it was often nec-essary to clothe descriptions in allegory and to borrow from human phraseology. Imperator added that things which are real to spirits would be imperceptible and impalpable to our crude senses. However, their surroundings are as real to them as ours are to us.

"In communicating to your mental plane ideas which are to you inconceivable, we are obliged to use expressions which are borrowed from your ways of thought," Imperator informed Moses. "We ourselves are very frequently at fault in misusing such expressions, or they are themselves inadequate to convey our meaning." [18]

When Moses was allowed to communicate with a friend recently passed, he asked him about the spheres. The friend told him that they are very similar, that they have flowers and fruits and pleasant landscapes, animals and birds. He said that he no longer craves food and that the only sustenance required is that drawn from the air he breathes. However, he added that explaining conditions to him is like (Moses) trying to explain earthly conditions to a deaf, dumb, and blind person.

"Our spirit dress would be imperceptible to you, and our spirit forms unrecognizable; consequently, we array ourselves in such sort as you would expect us to appear," the friend told Moses. "If the spirit is showing itself to its own friends, it would appear in the semblance of the dress it was in the habit of wearing in earth life; and would specially exaggerate, or draw attention to any peculiarity of gesture, dress or demeanor which would identify it." [19]

As mentioned above by Silver Birch and as discussed in Chapter IV, there are apparently souls who do not realize that they are "dead." This phenomenon was popularized in the hit movie, *The Sixth Sense*, a decade or so ago, when the Bruce Willis character didn't know he was dead until the end of the movie. No doubt many of the viewers of the movie assumed that it was nothing more than science fiction.

In his recent book, *To Die For*, Dr. James E. Beichler offers a framework by which to better understand the struggles between mind and consciousness, including why some spirits don't realize they are dead. "Mind interprets our sensed world and environment using reason, the cumulative result of real experiences of the material four-dimensional world placed within a specific mental framework or worldview," Beichler, a semi-retired physics professor, explains, "while consciousness deals more with intuition, our innate feelings and subconscious understanding of the larger five-dimensional framework of physical reality."

As Beichler sees it, when mind is much more evolved than consciousness those making the transition from this life to the larger life may be faced with a very big gap, thus not recognizing that they are dead. If the person had achieved a higher level of consciousness while occupying the physical body, "then the mind would already have memories of five-dimensional experience and would then merge with less difficulty into its new state of being," he explains, adding that this mind remains stuck in its four-dimensional reality.

In other words, the mind (the soul) separates itself from the physical organ (the brain) and then attempts to orientate itself based upon the spiritual consciousness that it has achieved during the time it occupied a physical shell. If the spiritual consciousness is well developed, the mind quickly awakens to its new and true reality. But if that consciousness is not well developed – if it is still grounded in the material world – this "handicapped" mind does not quickly "awaken" and may not even realize that the physical body has been shed, i.e., the soul doesn't realize that it is "dead."

"The mind/consciousness complex retains its identity (the person still remains) after a manner in the fifth dimension, in so far as self-identity is not a material but still a physical quantity or quality," Beichler further explains. "However, the extent to which the complex is 'conscious' or mindful of its own existence, its being, would depend upon the extent to which it was conscious' or aware of its five-dimensional connections before the death of the four-dimensional body and what is perceived by the mind as 'self' while the body still lived and functioned." [20]

Indications are that there are many degrees of awakening and consciousness on the Other Side and that many souls go back and forth over the threshold of awareness. That is, the conflict between mind and consciousness continues so that some souls realize at times that they have passed from the physical world but at other times they cling to the physical world and temporarily forget that they are "dead." They are in a struggle with earth's magnetism. The majority of souls may be in an in-between state, fluctuating back and forth over that threshold of awareness, "earthbound" at times and free from the "earthbound" condition at other times, however time is measured in that realm. Only those who are totally self-centered and materialistic in earth life don't realize their new state at all, at least initially.

Returning to the introductory paragraphs of this chapter, another perspective on this is to view the earth life like a movie, an illusory life, being viewed by the real self – the soul. During a movie, we occasionally remind ourselves that we are separate from the movie action, but we then again become absorbed by the action and feel much of the emotion being experienced by the actors. After a very emotionally-charged movie ends, it sometimes affects us for the rest of the day or evening. And so it seems to be with the soul that has a hard time shaking off the earth experiences.

Still another area that defies human understanding and invites scoffs from skeptics and debunkers is that of communication with the spirit world. Skeptics seem to assume that it should be as simple as a long-distance phone call, but we know from various messages received that there are many obstacles to communication with the spirit world. In many of the most evidential mediumistic settings, such as those involving Leonora Piper* and Gladys Osborne Leonard*, two of the most credible and celebrated mediums in history, there are four parties – the sitter and the human medium on this side and the spirit communicator and the spirit "control" on the other side. The spirit control is, in effect, a medium on the other side, interpreting what the spirit communicator wants to say, relaying it on through the earthly medium, who then interprets it and passes it on to the sitter. Indications are that there is often much distortion of messages in the process of converting thought images to words.

After his death in 1925, Sir William Barrett* began communicating with his wife, Lady Florence Barrett, a physician and dean of the women's college of medicine in London, through several mediums, including Mrs. Leonard. He told her that he had to learn how to slow down his vibration in order to communicate with her. "Sometimes I lose my memory of things from coming here," he continued. "I know in my own state but not here. In dreams you do not know everything, you only get parts in a dream. A sitting is similar; when I go back to the spirit world after a sitting like this I know I have not got everything through that I wanted to say. That is due to my mind separating again."

Initially, Lady Barrett was skeptical and asked for proof that the communicator was her late husband. Sir William responded by mentioning a tear in the wall paper in the corner of his room and a broken door knob, both of which they had discussed a month or so before his death, and the fact that they had now been repaired. This was especially evidential to Lady Barrett.

Sir William went on to explain that in the earth body we have the separation of subconscious and conscious and that when we pass over they join and make a complete mind that knows and remembers everything. However, when he brings himself back into the physical sphere, the conscious and the subconscious again separate and he forgets much. "I cannot come with my whole self, I cannot."

When Lady Barrett asked him to elaborate, Sir William pointed out that he has a fourth dimensional self which cannot make its fourth dimension exactly the same as the third. "It's like measuring a third dimension by its square feet instead of by its cubic feet," he continued, "and there is no doubt about it I have left something of myself outside which rejoins me directly when I put myself into the condition in which I readjust myself." [21]

At a later sitting, Sir William explained that when he was in his own sphere he would remember a name, but when he came into the conditions of a sitting he could not always remember it. "The easiest things to lay hold of are what we may call ideas," he communicated. "A detached word, a proper name, has no link with a train of thought except in a detached sense; that is far more difficult than any other feat of memory or association of ideas. If you go to a medium that is new to us, I can make myself known by giving you through that medium an impression of my character and personality, my work on earth, and so forth. Those can all be suggested by thought impressions, ideas; but if I want to say 'I am Will,' I find that is much more difficult than giving you a long, comprehensive study of my personality. 'I am Will' sounds so simple, but you understand that in this case the word 'Will' becomes a detached word." [22]

Sir William added that if he wanted to express an idea of his scientific interests he could do it in twenty different ways. He could begin by showing books, then giving impressions of the nature of the book and so on until he had built up a character impression of himself, but to simply say "I am Will" was a real struggle for him.

In 1917, Rev. Charles Drayton Thomas, a psychical researcher, began sitting with Gladys Osborne Leonard. He quickly made contact with his father, John D. Thomas, and his sister, Etta, receiving much veridical information to prove their identities. However, he wondered why they had such difficulty in giving their names and the names of others. It became evident that the giving of a name involved the overcoming of some obstacle, and that usually the difficulty, whatever it might be, was too serious to permit of success," Thomas wrote in his 1928 book, *Life Beyond Death with Evidence.* "There is unquestionably a difficulty in transmitting names through trance mediums, though some give them more successfully than do others."

With Leonard, the information was usually transmitted by Feda, her spirit control. That is, Leonard would go into a trance and Feda would take over her organism. Feda often spoke of herself in the third person, e.g., "Feda is having difficulty understanding."

The discarnate Thomas explained the difficulty to his son: "One cannot sometimes get the names right. If I wish to speak about a man named Meadow, I may try that name and find that Meadow is not spoken rightly by Feda. So I then wait and try to insert the idea of a green field, connecting it with the idea of the man described. We always try for a definite thing which will tell you exactly what we mean; but if unable to do that, we have to get as near to it as we can. Sometimes we have to depend upon slender links in giving you the clue."

As another example, the discarnate Thomas mentioned that when he tried to get the name Jerusalem through Feda, she gave the word "Zion" instead.

Etta explained to her brother that it was much easier to send ideas to Feda than it was to send words. She added that she could not get her husband's name, Whitfield, through Feda. "Is it not strange that I cannot say my husband's name?" she communicated. "I can feel it, but cannot say it; that is, I cannot get it spoken. I get it on the surface, so to speak, but cannot get it into the medium's mind." At a sitting four months later, Etta again attempted to get her husband's name through, but only succeeded in getting the medium to say, "Wh--, Whi---, Wht--."

Etta further told her brother that the more she tried to think on the name, the more difficult it was to get it through the medium's brain, adding that she could not control the medium's power of expression. "One may get a word into her mind and yet be unable to make her express it," she explained. "Because it is in the mind it does not follow that her brain will take it. Unless the ideas in the mind are tapped on to the actual brain one cannot express them."

Etta likened the brain of the medium to a keyboard on a typewriter. "You can place your finger on the right key, but unless you tap it there is no expression. The brain takes or does not take from the mind." Trying too much for a certain word, Etta continued, results in the keys becoming "stiff" with apprehension.

Thomas noticed that Feda could more easily catch a first syllable than the whole name, but sometimes she would catch only the first letter, which he understood was pictured for her by the communicator. One communicating entity tried to get the word Greek through, Feda struggled with "G--, Gre--, Grek, Greg, Greeg."[23]

In effect, the celestial world does not easily lend itself to analyses by using terrestrial methods and reasoning. Those desiring to understand the celestial world must open their minds and forget about applying only the five senses and known science.

[1] Swain, Jasper, *On The Death of My Son,* The Aquarian Press, UK, 1989, pp. 36-37

[2] Sculthorp, Frederick, *Excursions to the Spirit World,* The Greater World Assoc., London, 1961, p. 43

[3] Naylor, William, *Silver Birch Anthology,* Spiritualist Press, London, 1955, p. 56

4 _____ p. 59

5 Cummins, Geraldine, *The Road to Immortality*, The Aquarian Press, London, 1955, pp. 9-15

6 Lodge, Sir Oliver, *Raymond or Life and Death*, George H. Doran Co., New York, 1916, p. 189

7 Cummins, Geraldine, *The Road to Immortality*, The Aquarian Press, London, 1955, p. 49

8 Swedenborg, Emanuel, *Heaven & Hell*, Swedenborg Foundation, West Chester, PA, 1976, p. 139

9 Stead, William T. *After Death*, The Progressive Thinker Publishing House, Chicago, 1909, p. 38

10 Stead, William T., *The Blue Island*, Hutchinson & Co., London, 1922, p. 88

11 Medhurst, R. G., *Crookes and the Spirit World*, Taplinger Publishing, Inc. New York, 1972

12 Kelway-Bamber, L., *Claude's Book*, Psychic Book Club, London, p. 22

13 Tymn, Michael, *Are We Our Own Tailors?* Atlantis Rising Magazine, No. 73

14 Owen, G. Vale, *The Life Beyond The Veil*, George H. Doran Co., New York, 1921, p. 52

15 Rosher, Grace, *The Travellers' Return*, Psychic Press, Ltd., London, 1968, p. 61

16 Pole, Wellesley Tudor, *Private Dowding*, Pilgrims Book Service, Norwich, England, 1966, p. 25

17 Ford, Sarah Louise, *Interwoven*, The Progressive Thinker Publishing House, Chicago, 1907, p.102

18 Moses, William Stainton, *Spirit Teachings*, Arno Press, New York, 1976, p. 66

19 Moses, William Stainton, *More Sprit Teachings*, Meilach.com, Sec. II, p. 22

20 Beichler, James E., *To Die For*, Trafford Publishing, Victoria, Canada, 2008, pp. 273-280

21 Barrett, Lady, *Personality Survives Death*, Longman, Green and Co.,, London, 1937, pp 55-56

22 _____ p. 105

23 Thomas, Charles Drayton, *Life Beyond Death With Evidence*, W. Collins Sons & Co. Ltd., London, 1928, pp. 218--225

8

YOU DO TAKE IT WITH YOU

*As the soul lives in the earth-life, so does it go to
the spirit-life. Its tastes, its predilections, its habits, its antipathies, they are with it still.*

— **Imperator**

According to Sogyal Rinpoche, author of *The Tibetan Book of Living and Dying,* the ideal way for a person to die is to give away
everything, internally and externally, so that "there is as little as
possible yearning, grasping, and attachment for the mind at that essential moment to latch onto." [1]

While this may be the ideal way, it is not necessarily the most prac-
ticable way, especially for those who have spouses who must continue
to support themselves with the joint assets. Nevertheless, all indications are that we do take our earthly concerns, anxieties, regrets, addictions, obsessions and unfinished business with us to the afterlife
and therefore it behooves us to leave this life with as few unresolved
issues as possible.

Communicating through a medium, Dr. Frederic H. Wood asked
his discarnate mother how victims of drink fare in the afterlife. "The
craving goes over with the etheric body," his mother replied, "and it
goes over with the mind, too. Disease of that kind affects the whole
personality. It is true of other vices, too, and also the mental ones of
greed, malice, vanity, or selfishness. These become part of yourself

unless you conquer them."[2] She added that such addictions are some-times more difficult to eradicate on her side than on earth.

"The drunkard retains his old thirst, but exaggerated," Imperator told William Stainton Moses*, "aggravated by the impossibility of shaking it. It burns within him, the unquenched desire, and urges him to frequent the haunts of his old vices, and to drive wretches like himself to further degradation."[3] Imperator explained that such spirits hover around other drunkards and feed off them while further influencing them in their negative addiction.

In her 1999 book, *Freeing Captives,* Dr. Louise Ireland-Frey, tells how she moved from mainstream medicine to hypnotherapy and a belief in spirit attachment. As Ireland-Frey came to understand it, like attracts like and a deceased alcoholic may look for a living alcoholic to feed off of, while a deceased sex addict will look for someone with a similar tendency. Of course, mainstream psychiatry and psychology want nothing to do with something so "unscientific" as spirit influence or spirit attachment, but more and more credible mental health practitioners seem to be subscribing to the idea of spirit releasement therapy.

Communicating through Wellesley Tudor Pole, Thomas Dowding, a school teacher who died at age 37 during World War I, told of observing a newspaper editor who was so addicted to his work when alive in the flesh that he was unable to throw off earth conditions after dying and thus built himself an office filled with telephones and tape machines. "These machines are in a way illusory, but they please the old gentlemen," Dowding communicated, pointing out that the man's obsession with his work prevented him from understanding his condition and progressing.

"Take a bird's eye, dispassionate view of all your worldly interests," Dowding advised. "Master them or they will master you. In the latter case, when you get here, you will be miserable. Life will seem empty, a wilderness. Earth ties tighten their grip, yet you will be unable to respond. Confusion will result – that is purgatory."[4]

But the excess baggage we carry over into the afterlife may not be something so severe as alcoholism or an addiction to drugs, sex, or work. It might be a single act of indiscretion. Consider two stories related by Dr. Minot Savage, a prominent Unitarian minister and author. When Savage sat with Leonora Piper*, the famous Boston medium, he was told that his son, who had died at age 31 three years earlier, was present. "Papa, I want you go at once to my room," Savage recalled his son communicating with a great deal of earnestness. "Look in my drawer and you will find a lot of loose papers. Among them are some which I would like you to take and destroy at once."

The son had lived with a personal friend in Boston and his personal effects remained there. Savage went to his son's room and searched the drawer, gathering up all the loose papers. "There were things there which he had jotted down and trusted to the privacy of his drawer which he would not have made public for the world," Savage ended the story, commenting that he would not violate his son's privacy by disclosing the contents of the papers. [5]

As further reported by Savage and also recorded in the records of the American Society for Psychical Research (ASPR), the Rev. W. H. Savage, Minot's brother, sat with Piper on Dec. 28, 1888. Phinuit, Piper's spirit control, told him that somebody named Robert West was there and wanted to send a message to Minot. The message was in the form of an apology for something West had written about Minot "in advance." W. H. Savage did not understand the message but passed it on to Minot, who understood it and explained that West was editor of a publication called *The Advance* and had criticized his work in an editorial. During the sitting, W. H. Savage asked for a description of West. An accurate description was given along with the information that West had died of hemorrhage of the kidneys, a fact unknown to Savage but later verified.

"Now the striking thing about this lies in the fact that my brother was not thinking of this matter and cared nothing about it," Minot Savage ended the story, feeling that this ruled out mental telepathy on the part of the medium. "There was no reason for the [apology] unless it be found in simply human feeling on [West's] part that he had discovered that he had been guilty of an injustice, and wished, as far as possible, to make reparation, and this for peace of his own mind." [6]

A story similar to that of Savage's son was related some years earlier by Samuel Wilberforce, the Anglican Bishop of Winchester, during the latter part of the 19th Century. Wilberforce was told of a ghostly visitor at the home of a famous Catholic family not far from where he resided. This spirit form was said to appear in a monk's habit and seemed to be searching for something in the library. Highly skeptical, Wilberforce felt obligated to investigate. He called upon the family and was given permission to spend some time in the library during the night, apparently at the time the spirit was usually seen. After a while, Wilberforce observed a monk enter the room and begin searching among the books. Although the monk looked solid and real to Wilberforce, he vanished into nothing.

Wilberforce returned the following night at the same time to see if the monk would again appear. After a short wait, he observed the monk make his way to the bookcases and begin searching. Wilberforce decided to ask him what he was looking for. The monk replied that many years earlier he had hidden some papers in the bookcase that incriminated a former member of the family. This had weighed heavily on his mind and he did not want it to fall into anyone's hands. Wilberforce told the monk that he would assist him in finding the papers. After a long search, they found the papers, at which time the monk asked Wilberforce to burn them, which he did. The monk vanished and was never seen again.

"It is apparent that the thoughts and memories that the monk had before his death, such as his concerns about the papers, continued to exist in his mind after his death, and besides continued to cause him worry and anxiety about the good name of the person concerned," wrote Dr. B. J. F. Laubscher, a South African psychiatrist and psychical researcher.[7]

Still another story involving possibly embarrassing or incriminating papers left behind was told by Harvard professor William James. It involved Dr. Richard Hodgson, the researcher who studied Leonora Piper for some 18 years. After Hodgson's death in 1905, he began communicating with James and other researchers through Mrs. Piper. At a sitting with researcher John Piddington, Hodgson expressed concern about some old love letters he had exchanged with a woman he had once hoped to marry. Hodgson said he wasn't sure whether he had destroyed the letters or not and asked Piddington to search his files and destroy them if they still existed. Piddington was unable to find the letters, suggesting that Hodgson had destroyed them before his death, but the communication proved to be evidential in that neither he nor anyone else knew of Hodgson's proposal to the woman. When contact was later made with the woman, she confirmed that Hodgson had once proposed marriage to her.

Thomas Erskine, who served as Lord Chancellor of the United Kingdom during the early part of the 19th Century, recalled a time when he had arrived in Scotland after a long absence. Upon coming out of a bookshop in Edinburgh, he met his old family butler. "He looked greatly changed, pale, wan, and shadowy," Erskine related. When Erskine asked him what he was doing there, the man replied: "To meet your honour and to solicit your interference with my lord to recover a sum due to me, which the steward at the last settlement did not pay."

Erskine asked him to step back into the bookshop and further explain, but the old butler then vanished. Upon investigating, Erskine found out that the old man had died some months earlier and had told his wife before he died that Erskine's father's steward had wronged him of some money. The dying man assured his wife that "Master Tom" would right the situation upon his return to Scotland. "This I promised to do, and shortly after fulfilled my promise," Erskine ended the story. "The impression of this on me was indelible."[8]

There have been many other messages from the spirit world suggesting that unfinished business weighs heavily on the departed soul. One of the more famous cases involved a will left by James Chaffin, of South Carolina. In 1905, Chaffin drew up a will in which he left all his property to the third of four sons. However, 14 years later, he changed the will to distribute the property to all his sons. He placed the second will in his father's old Bible. When Chaffin died from a fall in 1921, the first will came into effect as no one knew of the second will.

In 1925, the second son had a "dream" in which his father appeared to him and told him to check his overcoat pocket. When the second son checked with his mother, he was told that the overcoat had been given to the oldest brother. The two oldest sons then found a piece of paper in their father's overcoat with the following instructions in their father's handwriting: "Read the 27th Chapter of Genesis in my Daddy's old Bible." When they found the old Bible and turned to the 27th Chapter of Genesis, they found the 1919 will. It was produced in court and admitted as genuine by Chaffin's widow and the brothers. The court then recognized the second will as the valid one.[9]

Another case involving a will arose out of the 1915 sinking of the *Lusitania* by a German U-boat. Sir Hugh Lane, an art connoisseur and director of the National Gallery of Ireland in Dublin, was transporting lead containers with paintings of Monet, Rembrandt, Rubens, and Titian, which were insured for $4 million and were to be displayed at the National Gallery. It was reported by survivors that Lane was seen on deck looking out to Ireland before going down to the dining saloon just before the torpedoes struck.

On the very night of the disaster, Hester Travers Smith and Lennox Robinson were sitting at a Ouija board in Dublin, Ireland. As was their usual practice, Travers Smith, the oldest daughter of Professor Edward Dowden, a Shakespearian scholar, and Robinson, a world-renowned Irish playwright, sat blindfolded at the board, their fingers lightly touching the board's "traveler," a triangular piece of wood which flies from letter to letter under the direction of a spirit control. They had experienced several controls over their years of operating the ouija board, but on this particular night the control was a spirit known to them as Peter Rooney. Rooney would be in touch with others on his side and deliver their messages for them if they lacked the experience to communicate on their own. Reverend Savell Hicks sat at the table between Travers Smith and Robinson, copying the letters indicated by the traveler.

"I am Hugh Lane, all is dark," was spelled out by the traveler, although Travers Smith and Robinson were blindfolded and had no clue as to the message. In fact, they were conversing on other matters as their hands moved rapidly. After several minutes, Hicks told Travers Smith and Robinson that it was Sir Hugh Lane coming through and that he told them he was aboard the *Lusitania* and had drowned.

While they had heard of the disaster, none of the three was aware that Lane was a passenger on the ship. They continued receiving messages from Lane, who told them that there was panic, the life boats were lowered, and the women went first. He went on to say that he was the last to get in an overcrowded life boat, fell over, and lost all memory until he "saw a light" at their sitting. To establish his identity, Lane gave Travers Smith an evidential message about the last time they had met and talked.

"I did not suffer. I was drowned and felt nothing," Lane further communicated through Peter Rooney that night. He also gave intimate messages for friends of his in Dublin.

Lane continued to communicate at subsequent sittings. As plans were underway to erect a memorial gallery to him, he begged that Travers Smith let those behind the movement know that he did not want such a memorial. However, he was more concerned that a codicil to his will would be honored. He had left his private collection of art to the National Gallery in London, but the codicil stated that they should go to the National Gallery in Dublin. Because he had not signed the codicil, the London gallery was reluctant to give them up. "Those pictures must be secured for Dublin," Lane communicated on January 22, 1918. "Tell them I cannot rise or get rest: it tortures me. Do you believe me? I am Hugh Lane!" [10]

At a sitting that September, Sir William Barrett, the distinguished British physicist and psychical researcher, was present. Prior to the sitting, Travers Smith and Barrett discussed how evidential the messages from Lane were to them, although they could understand why the public doubted. After the sitting started, a man who said he had died in Sheffield communicated first. Then, Travers Smith recalled, Robinson's arm was seized and driven about so forcibly that the traveler fell off the table more than once. It was Lane, who was upset because of the doubts expressed relative to his communication.

While not exactly in the category of unresolved issues, "The Pearl Tie-Pin Case" shows concern on the part of the spirit communicator. It also involved Hester Travers Smith, who was sitting at the ouija board with Geraldine Cummins*, the 17-year-old daughter of a physician, when the name of Cummins' cousin, an army officer killed in France a month earlier, was unexpectedly spelled out on the board. The following message then came: "Tell mother to give my pearl tie-pin to the girl I was going to marry, I think she ought to have it." As Cummins was unaware that her cousin had intended to marry and did not know the name of the woman, she asked that the name and address of the woman be given. The full Christian and surname was given on the board along with an address in London. Either the address was not accurately communicated or was taken down wrong, as a letter sent to that address was returned. Cummins checked with other family members and none was aware that the cousin had been engaged nor knew the fiancée named.

Several months later, the family of the young officer received his personal effects from the War Office. They included a pearl tie-pin along with a will naming the fiancée as his next of kin. Both the Christian and surname were exactly as given to Cummins, who would later develop into a world-famous medium and author.

Here, too, Sir William Barrett investigated, contacting Cummins and confirming the facts, including the fact that the message was recorded at the time and not written from memory. "Here there could be no explanation of the facts by subliminal memory, or telepathy, or collusion," Barrett wrote, "and the evidence points unmistakably to a telepathic message from the deceased officer." [11]

On November 10, 1928, Molly Ross sat with Geraldine Cummins in London. "Mo..Mo...Molly. I am here. I see you," Molly's deceased sister, Alice, communicated through Cummins' hand. "It's all true. I am alive. The pain went at once. I felt suffocating. Then, just after I got that awful choking, I felt things were breaking up all about me. I heard crackling like fire and then dimness. I saw you bending down with such a white face and you were looking at me, and I wasn't there."

Alice said that she regretted not having treated her second son, who was living in East Africa, as an equal to Ronald. (Molly confirmed that Ronald was her sister's favorite and that Ronald was favored in Alice's will.)

Another deceased sister, Margaret, took control of the pencil and said that Alice was having a hard time "managing the words." Margaret then communicated that Alice also regretted treating her husband badly. Molly noted that this was also very evidential as Alice "bullied her husband dreadfully."

Margaret then mentioned that Alice still resented the fact that Margaret cut her out of her will and left her share to Charles, their brother, who had no need of the money. This was another very evidential fact to Molly, as it was clearly unknown to the medium. "She hasn't forgotten yet the way I left my money," Margaret wrote. "She feels it would have made a difference in her last days."

Molly told Margaret that Alice's family was managing financially. "Good," Margaret replied. "I will tell her that, then she won't bother about things. The fact of the matter is, she came out of the world with a dark cloud of years of troubled thought about money. It all accumulated and clung about her. But I think now it will be slowly dissipated...All that worrying before her death left her in a very scattered state of mind." [12]

A rare coin, known as the "Widow's Mite," apparently caused some afterlife consternation. The story was related by Dr. Isaac Funk, a partner in the American company, Funk & Wagnalls, publishers of *The Standard Dictionary*.

During 1894, Funk borrowed the coin from Professor Charles West so that it could be illustrated in his company's dictionary. Henry Ward Beecher, a mutual friend, had told Funk about the coin and introduced him to West some years earlier. As Funk was to later recall, he gave the coin to his brother, Benjamin, the company's business manager, and asked him to return it to Professor West after the photographic plate was made. Benjamin then gave the coin, along with another coin, both in a sealed envelope to H. L. Raymond, head cashier of the company. Raymond placed the envelope in the drawer of a large combination safe, where it would remain forgotten for some nine years.

It was in February of 1903, after both West and Beecher had died, that Funk, a member of the American branch of the Society for Psychical Research, was told about an apparently gifted medium in Brooklyn. On his third visit to this medium, the medium's spirit control said that Beecher, who was unable to communicate directly, was concerned because of an ancient coin. "This coin is out of its place and should be returned," the message came through. "It has long been away, and Mr. Beecher wishes it returned, and he looks to *you*, doctor, to return it."[13]

Funk pressed for more information and was told that it was in a large iron safe in a drawer under a lot of papers. At his office the next day, Funk had the bookkeeper check the company safe. There, they found the coin in a little drawer in the safe under a lot of papers. The coin was then given to West's son.

Although Beecher was not responsible for holding on to the coin, he apparently felt some responsibility for it, or it may have been that West was unable to communicate and asked Beecher to remind Funk that it had not been returned.

A number of spirit messages have suggested that a departed soul can remain earthbound because of the grief of loved ones. Such was the message communicated by Olive Thomas, a popular Hollywood actress of the silent-screen era, who died of a medication overdose during September 1920.

Communicating with J. Gay Stevens, a New York journalist and a member of the American Society for Psychical Research, through medium Chester Michael Grady, Thomas informed Stevens that she needed to get word to her mother that her death was accidental, not a "scandalous suicide" as had been reported by the press. She explained that when she couldn't sleep she reached for a bottle of sleeping pills but took the wrong bottle, one very similar in appearance. It contained bichloride of mercury, which killed her.

When Stevens contacted Thomas' mother, the mother wanted nothing to do with him, assuming that, as a journalist, he was just trying to add to the scandal. But Olive Thomas pleaded for Stevens to make further efforts to convince her mother. Over a period of a dozen sittings, Thomas provided Stevens with personal information which had not been public knowledge, hoping that her mother would realize that she was in fact communicating. But the mother still resisted, concluding that as a journalist Stevens had special ways of gathering information. Moreover, her pastor told her that it must be the work of Satan.

Thomas insisted, however, that Stevens keep trying. She then provided some very evidential information which she felt certain would convince her mother that she was alive in the spirit world and communicating. She said that all of her jewelry had been returned to her mother after her death, except one item – her favorite brooch. She told

Stevens that the brooch got caught up in the lining of a pocket in the steamer trunk now in her mother's attic. She also told Stevens that one of the pearls, the third from the top on the right, had come out of its setting and was loose in the tissue paper surrounding the brooch.

After Stevens brought this information to Thomas' mother, the mother reluctantly agreed to go to the attic and search the steamer trunk. Finding the brooch with the loose pearl was enough to convince her that her daughter, not Satan, was actually communicating. She accepted the explanation that her daughter did not commit suicide and this apparently relieved much of her grief and also gave Olive a certain peace of mind. [14]

When Alice Gilbert asked her deceased son Philip about carrying over one's interest in such things as music, art, and cricket, to the afterlife, Philip gave a "yes and no," telling her it was very difficult to explain. "If anyone has got anything on his mind, an obsession for, say, cricket, he will live in an illusion world of that, and will not attain his full power and knowledge of how to get on here till he has snapped out of it and that may take centuries [in earth time]," Philip explained, further pointing out that any activity which depends for its impetus on physical body skill, such as sport or even investing in the stock market, has no equivalent in the reality there. However, such activities as music, art, and mathematics can be continued there as they are universal activities that extend from the afterlife realms to earth. [15]

There are many other stories suggesting that we take our concerns, anxieties, mistakes, obsessions, and regrets with us to the afterlife, including more than a few in which the communicators said that their biggest regret was not learning more about the afterlife when they were alive in the flesh. When Allan Kardec tried to invoke a Mr. Van Durst, an old acquaintance, he was told by the medium's spirit control that Van Durst was still in a state of confusion and was unable to communicate. When Kardec eventually made contact, Van Durst said that his state of confusion would have been shorter and less painful if he had been more concerned with the spiritual when he was alive. "You strive to regain the consciousness of your *me*, and you cannot grasp it," he communicated his initial awareness. "You no longer exist, and yet you feel that, nevertheless, you *do* exist, but in what an abyss of confusion and trouble! And presently, after a lapse of time that you are unable to measure, a time of *latent* distress – for you have no longer the strength to feel it understandingly – after this lapse of time which seems to you interminable, to be slowly reborn into existence, to wake up in a new world!...

"But, if, before quitting the earth, I had known what you know, how much more easy and agreeable would have been my initiation into this other life." [16]

[1] Rinpoche, Sogyal, *The Tibetan Book of Living and Dying*, HarperSan Francisco, 1993, p. 224

[2] Wood, Frederic H , *Through the Psychic Door*, Psychic Book Club, London, 1954, p. 67

[3] Moses, William Stainton, *Spirit Teachings*, Arno Press, New York, 1976, p.24

[4] Pole, Wellesley Tudor, *Private Dowding*, Pilgrim Book Services, Norwich, England, 1966, pp. 23-24

[5] Savage, Minot, *Can Telepathy Explain?*, G. P. Putnam's Sons, New York, 1902, pp. 106-107

[6] _____ pp. 121-122

[7] Laubscher, B. J. F., *Beyond Life's Curtain*, Neville Spearman, Jersey, UK, 1975, pp. 19-20

[8] Tweedale, Charles L., *Man's Survival After Death*, The Psychic Book Club, London, 1909, pp. 166-167.

[9] Crookall, Robert, *Intimations of Immortality*, James Clarke & Co., Ltd., UK, 1965, p. 57

[10] Smith, Hester Travers, *Voices From The Void*, E.P. Dutton & Co., New York, 1919, pp. 49-55

[11] Barrett, Sir William, *On the Threshold of the Unseen*, E. P. Dutton & Co., New York, 1918, pp. 184-186

[12] Cummins, Geraldine, *They Survive*, Psychic Book Club, London, no date, pp. 93-123

[13] Funk, Isaac K., *The Widow's Mite and Other Psychic Phenomena*, Funk and Wagnalls, New York, 1911, pp. 157-169

[14] Stevens, J. Gay, *The Girl with the Golden Hair*, FATE Magazine, Dec. 1972, Jan. 1973

[15] Gilbert, Alice, *Philip in the Spheres*, The Aquarian Press, London, 1952, p. 21

[16] Kardec, Allan, *Heaven and Hell*, Trubner & Co., London, 1878, pp. 225-226 .

9

FINDING MEANING

Your world must realize that revelation is contin-
uous and progressive, fitting itself to the stage of
understanding to the people to whom it comes.
— **Silver Birch**

Unfortunately, much of the discussion of the afterlife by spirit communicators has to do with the lower spheres, where we are told
that many souls remain "earthbound," clinging desperately to their
earthly ways and interests. Such a scenario doesn't do much more to
inspire the materialistic person still in the earth life than that of the
afterlife picture offered by orthodox religions. It is still something to
fear, even if not quite as horrific as the orthodox afterlife.

The primary reason we know more about the lower spheres, we are
told by spirit communicators, is that they more closely resemble earth
conditions and thus are easier to describe or put into language. Conditions on the middle and higher spheres are said to be increasingly
beyond human language and comprehension. Nevertheless, we are assured, they are increasingly desirable.

"After I had rested for a little while, I felt like a boy on a holiday ex-
ploring a new wonderful place of which I had heard and conjectured
and pictured, but which more than came up to my expectations," Sir
William Barrett* communicated to his widow through the mediumship of Gladys Osborne Leonard*.

When Lady Barrett asked him if he thought she would like it when it was her time to cross over to that side, Sir William replied: "Yes, you *will*, you *will*. You like any place with possibilities. When you find yourself in a mental or physical cul-de-sac, you don't like it, but you'll *love* it here – you'll love it. To me it's a perfect condition."[1]

Also communicating through the trance-mediumship of Gladys Osborne Leonard, John Thomas, who said he was on the third plane, told his son, Charles Drayton Thomas, that his spirit body was so much more powerful than his physical body. "I wish to emphasize that not only am I surrounded by greater beauty and happiness, but that my powers of appreciation are greatly expanded," he added. "You know how one used to walk past beautiful flowers, and grand sights, without seeing all that was in them; we are able to see the complete beauty. In short, our powers are a thousand times greater than yours."

Etta, Drayton Thomas's deceased sister, said that she was experiencing all the things she had missed in her earth life. "When you come here you will find that which is difficult for me to express," she said. "You will realize the good of what you have done, and the happiness which you had, and, beyond that, also the happiness which you might have had, and which, just because you might have had it, it is still yours. This will include things which were apparently taken from you, but which you let go willingly and not grudgingly; for those things you have made doubly, nay trebly, your own."[2]

Gordon Burdick communicated to Grace Rosher that he thought he was dreaming when he was greeted after his physical death by his mother and brother. "It is a world in many ways similar to the one we have left," Burdick stated through Rosher, "but far more beautiful, as there is nothing to damage or destroy. All our activity is controlled by thought. We realize that the power of thought is the greatest force. Right thinking is the most potent force there is to combat all the so-called horror of evil."[3]

In one of the classics of spirit communication, *The Bridge Over the River*, Sigwart, a promising young musician killed in World War I, communicated extensively with his sister after his death. "I am more alive than ever before and can sense everything," he told her. "When thoughts of sadness over my departure reappear, you cannot hide them from me. My feelings are more alert in such moments because I perceive with my highest ego, while everything is veiled for you by matter. We also experience still the sensation of weeping, but only when facing moments of greatness."

Sigwart added that he can work on whatever he enjoys. "You can hardly imagine what this means here; free of the fetters of earth; free of every material worry; free of the longing for an earthly body; freed from the sorrow of the bereaved. I am indescribably fortunate. Now I can work on all the thoughts I am harboring within me."[4]

Harvard professor William James, one of the pioneers of both psychology and psychical research, is said to have communicated through several credible mediums after his death in 1910, one of them Susy Smith. "Life after death, when experienced properly from the outset, is so challenging and so marvelously engrossing that life on earth is nothing in comparison," James communicated to Smith. "I can truthfully say that when you come to this sphere, you will find so much to interest and excite you that I cannot make it sound attractive enough."[5]

Silver Birch, the high spirit who communicated through the trance mediumship of Maurice Barbanell*, explained that it is especially difficult for those in the earth life to comprehend the higher spirit life because of the time factor. He said that in the lower spheres, time has a different meaning than in the higher spheres. "There is plenty of activity connected with the mind and spirit," he continued. "The difficulty [the human] has is in understanding spiritual experiences in terms of physical measurement, but there are wide and boundless pursuits of the mind and spirit, cultural, educational, purposive, actual in their effect on your physical world, to engage us and occupy us for as long as we wish to be occupied."[6]

As earlier discussed, and in summary, some spirit communicators have attempted to number the spheres in their efforts to make it more understandable to us. It appears the lowest sphere is comprised of the earthbound souls, most of whom don't seem to fully comprehend the fact that they have "died." Souls at this level apparently did very little during their lifetimes to develop any spiritual consciousness and contented themselves with living selfish and materialistic lifestyles, perhaps even depraved ones. This lowest or first level is what religions call "Hell," but it is not an eternal state.

The second sphere is populated by souls who developed a modicum of spiritual consciousness during their lifetimes but still, for the most part, led selfish and materialistic lives. Also, souls from the first sphere may have gained a little consciousness and advanced to this level after some time, however time is measured in that state. Although partially conscious, souls at this level are in something of a stupor, aware that they have "died" but still very confused or bewildered, yet more easily educated by missionary spirits from higher spheres.

Referred to by Spiritualists as "Summerland," the third sphere is said to be the one where the average decent person – one who has led a relatively good life even though still grounded in materialism and lacking in significant spiritual consciousness – finds him- or herself after separating from the physical body. He or she will be reunited with loved ones and will experience conditions very similar to those on the earth plane. It has been referred to as a "dream life," but less of a dream life than was experienced on the earth plane. Many will continue to practice their old religions at this level, but missionary spirits from even higher spheres will slowly wean them away from their limited beliefs and toward a more unified belief system.

The fourth sphere seems to be the abode for those with more than average spiritual consciousness when alive in the flesh. That is, they were less grounded in materialism and more interested in service to fellow humans than serving oneself. Also, souls from the third sphere may have advanced to this level. While the fourth sphere is mostly beyond human comprehension, conditions in the fifth, sixth, and seventh spheres are reportedly far beyond human comprehension and vocabulary.

Indications are that most spirit communicators reside on the third and fourth spheres. It has often been pointed out that the higher the sphere, the more difficult it is for spirits to communicate with those on earth because it becomes increasingly difficult to lower one's vibrations to the earth vibration as one advances. However, some highly advanced souls, such as Silver Birch and Imperator, both quoted several times in this book, were able to communicate in spite of the difficulties of lowering the vibration level, just as some people in the earth life seem to be better able to raise their vibrations than others. They said that it was necessary for them to relay messages through other spirits on lower spheres. Moreover, the messages suggest that the more spiritually conscious the medium, the easier it is for spirits from higher realms to communicate through him. William Stainton Moses*, the medium for Imperator, and Maurice Barbanell*, the medium for Silver Birch, seem to have been highly spiritual during their earth lives, thus facilitating communication, even if a go-between was required to relay the messages through them.

"The longer you have lived in our world, the further you are divorced from your world and the ties have become more or less sundered," Silver

Birch explained. "I had attained some degree of spiritual growth in that time, and a call was made for many of us to return to help your world, to teach some of the eternal verities, simple truths, principles, which had been forgotten, overlaid, which lay buried beneath a debris of falsity, superstition, ignorance, misconception, and prejudice."

Silver Birch went on to explain that in reducing his rate of vibration to communicate with those on earth he had to sacrifice some of his individuality, "for the nearer you come to earth, the less of the real you, the spiritual you, can be made manifest, and in order to achieve communication with your world I had to use a medium between my state of existence and yours."[7]

Imperator told Stainton Moses much the same thing and explained that low-level spirits, being closer to the earth vibration, will sometimes impersonate higher spirits and retard their work with falsehoods. The ability of the low-level spirits to do this depends on the character of the medium – the more spiritually conscious the medium, the more difficult it is for the low-level spirits to communicate through him or her. "For the present, we tell you that there are spirits who delight in such personation, and who have the power, under certain conditions, of carrying out elaborate deception," Imperator advised. "Such take names which they see to be desired, and would reply equally to any name given them. They may usually be excluded by a careful attention to conditions, and by the efforts of a strong guardian who is able to protect the circle."[8]

Being a priest of the Anglican Church, Moses found it difficult to accept some of the things Imperator told him as they seemingly conflicted with what he had been taught. He wondered how he could know that the messages he was receiving were not from some low-level spirit. Imperator praised Moses for questioning his words and not accepting everything he had to say. "We hail your doubts as the best evidence of our successful dealing with you," Imperator said. "We welcome your arguments as the intelligent proof that you have seen the full proportions of the claims we make as the messengers of the Most High."[9] Imperator advised him to use the standards of judgment set up by Jesus – "By their fruits ye shall know them" and "Men do not gather grapes of thorns, or figs of thistles." He suggested that Moses consider the whole tenor of his teachings as proof that it is Divine and told him that he could only dimly symbolize truths which one day Moses would be able to see in full splendor with unclouded eyes.

"We do say, we have always said, that man's responsibility is in proportion to the light which is in him," Imperator continued, "that man's duty is not lessened but increased by the quality of the revelation of which he is the recipient. We tell you that many a soul has progressed in spite of its creed by honesty and sincerity and singleness of purpose, and that many a soul has been dragged down by the very load of that faith in which its hopes were centered." [10]

But what is the meaning of it all? The more advanced spirits tell us that it is all about expanding consciousness, thereby progressing through the higher and higher states of vibration referred to as spheres. "The true attitude of the spirit is one of striving earnestly in the hope of reaching a higher position than that which it has attained," Imperator stated. "In perpetually progressing it finds its truest happiness. There is no finality; none, none, none!" [11]

Silver Birch explained that progression is constant through the spheres of consciousness and that earth provides a variety of learning experiences not available in the spirit world. "The whole object of earthly life is to have a variety of experiences that will fit the spirit for the next stage beyond earth when you have to pass into our world," he said, further explaining that progress can be "quickened" by the earth experience. Many souls, however, in exercising their free will, make wrong choices, thus failing to make significant progress during their earth experiences.

"You must be sharpened, purged, refined," Silver Birch continued. "You must experience the heights and the depths. You must have the variety of experiences that earth provides for you." [12]

As Silver Birch is quoted at the end of Chapter 6, the ultimate is not the attainment of Nirvana; it is progress toward increasing individuality. "As awareness increases," Silver Birch said, "the individual realizes that he or she possesses infinite possibilities, that the road to perfection is an endless one." [13]

It is all extremely difficult, if not impossible, for the human intellect to process. As Imperator mentioned, we can bewilder ourselves in our efforts to understand all of this, to define the indefinable. For now, we must be satisfied with knowing that consciousness survives physical death and that as we advance through higher and higher spheres, we find greater and greater fulfillment and joy. It is an active, vibrant, dynamic and *real* life, not the static humdrum Heaven of orthodox religion.

[1] Barrett, Florence, *Personality Survives Death*, Longmans, Green & Co., London, 1937, p. 30

[2] Thomas, Charles, *Drayton, Life Beyond Death With Evidence*, W. Collins Sons & Co., London, 1928, pp.178-184

[3] Rosher, Grace, *The Travellers' Return*, Psychic Press Ltd., London, 1968, p. 61.

[4] Wetzel, Joseph, *The Bridge Over the River*, Anthroposophic Press, 1974, pp. 92-93

[5] Smith, Susy, *The Book of James*, G. P. Putnam's Sons, New York, 1974, p. 41

[6] Naylor, William, *Silver Birch Anthology*, Spiritualist Press, London, 1955, p. 62

[7] Ortzen, Tony, *The Seed of Truth*, The Spiritual Truth Press, Surrey, UK, 1987, pp. 112-113

[8] Moses, William Stainton, *Spirit Teachings*, Arno Press, New York, 1976, p. 240

[9] _____ pp. 81-82.

[10] _____ p. 226

[11] _____ p. 157

[12] Ballard, Stan A. & Green, Roger, *Silver Birch Book of Questions & Answers*, Spiritual Truth Press, London, 1998, p. 147

[13] _____ p. 49

EPILOGUE

CUI BONO?

Inquiry into survival, and into the kind of experience through which we shall certainly have to go in a few years, is therefore eminently sane, and may be vitally significant. It may colour all our actions, and give a vivid meaning both to human history and to personal experience.

— **Sir Oliver Lodge**

C*ui Bono?* the skeptic asks. What good is it to know about the nature of the afterlife? Shouldn't we be focusing on this life?

Those two questions were addressed in the Preface of this book, but it seems appropriate, in light of what has been discussed in the preceding nine chapters, to briefly re-examine the answers in closing the book.

"It has always been to me a matter of surprise that people, who on religious grounds claim to believe in the survival of death, are apparently content to hold vague and unsatisfactory views about the nature of the life they will confront," wrote Dr. Raynor C. Johnson, Master of Queen's College, University of Melbourne, in his 1957 book, *Nurslings of Immortality.* "If they knew that in a few years' time they would be going to live permanently in another country, they would take an intelligent interest in learning what they could of that country." [1]

Johnson surmised that the reason most people do not attempt to find out more about their ultimate destination is a deep-seated repressed aversion to the irrevocable event called death. Moreover, he doubted that the average churchman has any clear views of the next life beyond formless spirits floating about in an indescribable heaven, and saw this indifference by the clergy as the source of funeral gloom.

As I, the author, see it, nothing has really changed since Professor Johnson wrote those words more than 50 years ago. If anything we have become more materialistic and hedonistic. Orthodox religion has been unable to stem the tide because it refuses to open itself up to modern revelation. It has not been able to offer us anything to visualize beyond streets of gold and angels with harps. Meanwhile, scientific fundamentalists dismiss all things spiritual as religious superstition. As a result, we continue in a downward spiral when it comes to the development of spiritual consciousness, the consciousness we most sorely need when we depart this world.

"We receive, day after day, the misfits, the derelicts, the outcasts, the flotsam and the jetsam, the millions who come here <u>unprepared</u>, <u>unready</u>, <u>unequipped</u> and who have to learn all over again," Silver Birch communicated. "Instead of passing to our world a stream of evolved souls ready to take up the tasks that await them, there come millions who have to be treated and nursed and tended because they are like bruised little children." [2] (emphasis added)

According to Silver Birch and many other spirit communicators, the key to being *prepared, ready,* and *equipped* for the *real* life is coming to understand it in this life. By no means did Silver Birch intend to imply that we should be more focused on the afterlife than on the one we are living. He put it in the words of Jesus, saying we should be *in* the world but not *of* the world. We should, he added, strive for balance between the physical world and the spiritual world.

Sir Oliver Lodge*, the distinguished British physicist, recognized the possibility of becoming overly absorbed in afterlife concerns and thereby missing out on the training of the present life. "But although we may rightly decide to live with full vigour in the present, and do our duty from moment to moment, yet in order to be full-flavoured and really intelligent beings – not merely with mechanical drift following the line of least resistance – we ought to be aware that there is a future – a future determined to some extent by actions in the present; and it is only reasonable that we should seek to ascertain, roughly and approximately, what sort of future it is likely to be." [3]

Imperator told William Stainton Moses* that his earthly work must be accomplished even at the risk of preventing the education of his spirit, but he added that Moses could eliminate many mundane and unnecessary earthly activities and thereby easily make room for more spiritual teachings and pursuits. He admonished Moses for spending too much time searching for objective evidence of God and the afterlife. "Faith to be real must be outside the limits of caution, and be fired by something more potent and effective than calculating prudence, or logical deductions, or judicial impartiality," Imperator told him. "It must be the fire that burns within, the mainspring that regulates the life, the overmastering force that will not be at rest. This is the faith that Jesus spoke of when He said of it that it was able to move mountains. This is that which braves death and torture, braces up feeble knees for long and hard endurance, and conducts its possessor safe at last through any perils that may assail him to the goal where faith finds its reward in fruition." [4]

At the very foundation of such faith is a belief that consciousness will survive death, that we will live on in another dimension. But that foundation easily crumbles when rational minds are unable to wrap their brains around an afterlife, when they are unable to visualize a non-material world. Modern revelation, as has come to us through credible mediumship, near-death experiences, and other paranormal phenomena over the past 160 years, gives us something to visualize, and once we are able to visualize it, even though fuzzy and not in complete focus, the Divine plan begins to unfold and make sense.

During December 1922, Sir Arthur Conan Doyle, the renowned British author, began receiving messages from a spirit called Pheneas, said to be a high soul who died thousands of years earlier. Among the messages Pheneas communicated was one in which he said that for the sake of future generations, a new right understanding of God is necessary. "Love, not fear, must reign in each heart," Pheneas stated. "Humanity must know the kind of existence they will lead in the lower greyer spheres if their lives are selfish and evil in the earth plane. Knowledge of where a man's actions are leading him will help and inspire him to live at his highest and what to avoid. The knowledge of the real and human happiness in the higher worlds ahead will give a man courage in facing sorrows and difficulties on this earth. The hope and joy of great happiness and the fulfillment of all his heart's ideals will make life here so much easier to bear, and so much more radiant." [5]

There is a very big difference between the lower spheres referred to by Pheneas and the Hell of orthodoxy. Understanding the difference can help bring rational minds back to belief and faith.

As Allan Kardec* came to see it after hearing from many advanced spirits, man's *real* life is in the soul and as long as he remains attached to external things and fancies that this world is all there is, he eventually abandons himself to despair. "In proportion as man arrives at a true comprehension of the future state, his fear of death diminishes," Kardec offered, "but as, at the same time, he also comprehends more clearly the uses of the earthly life, he awaits its ending calmly, without impatience or regret. The certainty of a future life gives another direction to his thoughts, another aim to his activities."

Such a comprehension, Kardec added, significantly mitigates the grief involved with the death of loved ones, since there is a certainty that we will meet up with them again, and also helps us endure the other hardships of this world. "The certainty of again meeting friends whom he has lost by death, of preserving the relationships he has formed upon the earth, of not losing the fruit of any effort, of continuing, forever, to grow in intelligence and in goodness, gives him patience to await the appointed term of his earthly sojourn, and courage to bear, unmurmuringly, the momentary fatigues and disappointments of terrestrial life," is how Kardec put it. [6]

Perhaps Mozart summed it up best when, near the end of his life, he wrote to his father: "Since death [properly understood] is the true ultimate purpose of our life I have for several years past made myself acquainted with this truest and best friend of mankind so that he has for me not only nothing terrifying any more but much that is tranquilising and consoling!....death...[is] the key to our true blessedness." [7]

[1] Johnson, Raynor C., *Nurslings of Immortality*, Harper & Brothers, New York, 1957, p. 240

[2] Storm, Stella, *Philosophy of Silver Birch*, Psychic Press, London, 1969, p. 154

[3] Lodge, Oliver, *Raymond or Life and Death*, George H. Doran Co., New York, 1916, p. 313

[4] Moses, William Stainton, *Spirit Teachings*, Arno Press, New York, 1976, p. 247

[5] Doyle, Arthur Conan, *Pheneas Speaks*, George H. Doran Co., New York, 1927, pp. 194-195

[6] Kardec, Allan, *Heaven and Hell*, Trubner & Co., London, 1878, p. 13

[7] Beard, Paul, *Living On*, Continuum, New York, 1981, p. 4

APPENDIX A

PRECOGNITION OR PREMONITIONS OF DEATH

In her intriguing 2010 book, *Messages,* Bonnie McEneaney, the wife of one of the victims of 9/11, tells of her husband having some kind of subconscious premonitions that his days were numbered. "I'm going to die before you," Eamon McEneaney told her in a somewhat matter-of-fact manner on September 4, 2001, a week before the terrorist attacks on the World Trade Center, where Eamon worked in mortgage-backed securities. Bonnie McEneaney says that her husband always believed that he would die young and, in the weeks preceding the disaster, seemed to have a sense that something monumental was imminent.[1]

Monica Iken, the wife of Michael Patrick Iken, another 9/11 victim, told McEneaney that her husband began acting a little strangely during the summer of 2001. When they received an invitation for a December wedding, Michael told Monica that he couldn't see himself being there. Around September 1, Michael's behavior became even more abnormal. When, on September 10, Monica told Michael that she was planning to visit a sick family member in New York City the following day, Michael became upset and told her not to go to the city that day.

Bonnie McEneaney further tells of Welles Crowther, a 24-year-old equities trader who died in the attack. His friends and family noticed that he began acting very strangely during the summer of 2001. He was described by friends and family as being "depressed," and "restless," and, on Labor Day, his mother remembered that he seemed very "melancholy," which was not characteristic of him.

A woman named Lorraine told McEneaney that she had a dream a week or so before 9/11 that seemed to suggest that her husband, Bill, would meet with a tragedy. She didn't tell her husband about the dream, but she also observed that Bill's behavior and attitude the weekend before 9/11 were very different from what they normally were.

A recent rerun of the Lisa Williams show on TV featured the parents of an 11-year-old boy who was killed in a boating accident off Waikiki in Hawaii. There was much evidential information passed on through Williams, a medium, to the parents, including the fact verified by his father that he did not want to go on the boat but was more or less forced into it by the parents. Williams told the parents that their son knew beforehand that he was going to die soon. When Williams mentioned this, the mother told her that after they returned home following their son's death, they found that their son left a message for them that he expected to be dying soon and looked forward to seeing his parents after they crossed over.

A December 7, 2007 Associated Press story tells of a Minnesota man, Fidel Sanchez-Flores, who died of an accidental death on his job. A week before his death he told his niece "to pray really hard" because "something is approaching." The day before his death he told his wife that he loved her and would continue to love her after his death. When his wife asked why he was saying that, he replied that he didn't know.

In his 1974 book, *On the Death of My Son,* Jasper Swain, a Republic of South Africa lawyer, tells of the death of his son Mike in an auto accident and the communications he received from Mike through several mediums. "My death was okayed well ahead of the accident," Mike told his father at one sitting. "To be exact, on the previous Monday, while I was watching the races at Kyalami, I suddenly knew that my life was coming to an end, even though I did not know the exact moment. I didn't regret it, because I was also aware of the wonder, the love, and the beauty of the world that awaited me." [2]

The story of President Abraham Lincoln's precognitive dream of his own death is well documented. One evening, about a month before his assassination, Lincoln sat in the White House with his wife Mary and several others when the subject of dreams came up. When Lincoln said something to the effect that there may be something to dreams, Mary asked him to elaborate on his beliefs. With some reluctance, Lincoln then related his prophetic dream. "About ten days ago, I retired late," he began the story. "I had been up waiting for important dispatches from the front. I could not have been long in bed when I fell into a slumber, for I was weary. I soon began to dream. There seemed to be a deathlike stillness about me. Then I heard subdued sobs, as if a number of people were weeping. I thought I left my bed and wandered downstairs."

As Lincoln, in his dream, wandered around downstairs, he continued to hear sobbing, but he could see no mourners. In fact, he saw no one. Lincoln was puzzled and alarmed at hearing the sobbing but seeing nobody. He continued walking until he reached the East Room, where he saw a catafalque, one which rested a corpse wrapped in funeral vestments. Around it were soldiers posted as guards. Lincoln then asked one of the soldiers who had died. "The President," was his answer, "He was killed by an assassin." A loud burst of grief from the crowd awakened Lincoln, who could not sleep the rest of the night.[3]

After Lincoln told of his dream to his wife and the others, Mary Lincoln was horrified, but Lincoln assured her that it was only a dream and suggested they forget about it.

Renowned French astronomer Camille Flammarion wrote about the dream of Edwin Reed, director of the Museum of Natural History in the city of Concepción, Chile. Two months before his death, Reed had a dream in which he saw a tomb with a cross on it with the following inscription: "Reed, naturalist, November 7, 1910" Reed jokingly related the strange dream to several friends, all of whom apparently shared in the humor of it until Reed died on November 7, 1910.[4]

There are countless stories similar to those mentioned here, all suggesting that the soul, or the higher self, becomes aware of the fact that it will soon depart the earth plane. It may be that the more spiritually evolved the person, the greater the awareness.

[1] McEneaney, Bonnie, *Messages*, Harper Collins Books, New York, 2010, pp. 19-22

[2] Swain, Jasper, *On the Death of my Son*, Turnstone Press, Northhamptonshire, England, 1974, p. 33

[3] Martinez, Susan B., *The Psychic Life of Abraham Lincoln*, New Page Books, Franklin Lakes, NJ., 2007, pp. 230-231

[4] Flammarion, Camille, *Death and Its Mystery: Before Death*, T. Fisher Unwin, Ltd., London, 1922

APPENDIX B

REINCARNATION

My pursuit of a spiritual path began with the works of Edgar Cayce, the famous American healer who, during trance, often tapped into the "Akashic Record" to examine a person's past lives and the relationship of his or her current afflictions to those lives.

After reading Dr. Ian Stevenson's *Twenty Cases Suggestive of Reincarnation* and psychiatrist Brian Weiss' *Many Lives, Many Masters*, I pretty much accepted reincarnation as fact. But then I read Swedenborg and was puzzled that he only alluded to reincarnation and was very vague on the subject. I moved on to *A Course in Miracles* and read, "In the ultimate sense, reincarnation is impossible. There is no past or future, and the idea of rebirth into a body has no meaning either once or many times."

Intriguing books by Rosemary Brown (*Unfinished Symphonies*), Suzy Smith (*The Book of James*) and Betty Eadie (*Embraced By The Light*) rejected reincarnation, at least in the way most people think of it. "Reincarnation, as usually understood, does not really happen," the spirit of the great composer Franz Liszt purportedly told Brown. "The truth is subtly different from the teachings of a reincarnationist on earth." [1]

Thus, there seemed to be strong evidence for reincarnation but, at the same time, seemingly credible mystics and spirit communicators were saying, or so I interpreted them, that it's not so. I didn't know what to believe.

Then I found the books of Silver Birch, the spirit entity who spoke through the entranced Maurice Barbanell of England for nearly 50 years.

"You will find that the higher the ascent in the spiritual scale, the more recognition is there that there is reincarnation," Silver Birch communicated, "but not in the facile form that is so often propounded." [2]

Silver Birch explained that the individual personality on earth is a small part of the individuality to which he or she belongs. He likened it to a diamond with its many facets, pointing out that the personality on earth is but one facet of the diamond. "What you express on earth is but an infinitesimal fraction of the individuality to which you belong. Thus there are what you call 'group souls,' a single unity with facets which have spiritual relationships that incarnate at different times, at different places, for the purpose of equipping the larger soul for its work." [3]

Silver Birch also likened the soul to an iceberg in which one small portion is manifesting and the greater portion not manifesting. He apparently was referring to what others have called the "Higher Self," the "Greater Self," or the "Oversoul." Trying to explain reincarnation to humans, Silver Birch added, is like trying to explain the color of the sky to someone who has been blind from birth.

The group-soul concept had earlier been advanced by the discarnate Frederic Myers through the mediumship of Geraldine Cummins. "When I was on earth, I belonged to a group-soul, but its branches and the spirit – which might be compared to the roots – were in the invisible," Myers, one of the pioneers of psychical research before his death in 1901, communicated. "Now, if you would understand psychic evolution, this group-soul must be studied and understood. For instance, it explains many of the difficulties that people will assure you can be removed only by the doctrine of reincarnation. You may think my statement frivolous, but the fact that we do appear on earth to be paying for the sins of another life is, in a certain sense, true. It is our life and yet not our life. In other words, a soul belonging to the group of which I am a part lived that previous life which built up for me the framework of my earthly life, lived it before I had passed through the gates of birth."

Myers further explained that the group soul might contain twenty souls, a hundred, or a thousand. "The number varies," he said. "It is different for each man. But what the Buddhist would call the karma I had brought with me from a previous life is, very frequently, not that of my life, but of the life of a soul that preceded me by many years on earth and left for me the pattern which made my life. I, too, wove a pattern for another of my group during my earthly career."

Myers added that the Buddhist's idea of rebirth, of man's continual return to earth, is but a half-truth. "And often half a truth is more inaccurate than an entire misstatement. I shall not live again on earth, but a new soul, one who will join our group, will shortly enter into the pattern or karma I have woven for him on earth." [4]

Myers likened the soul to a spectator caught within the spell of some drama outside of its actual life, perceiving all the consequences of acts, moods, and thoughts of a kindred soul. He further pointed out that there are an infinite variety of conditions in the invisible world and that he made no claim to being infallible. He called it a "general rule" based on what he had learned and experienced on the Other Side.

In 1918, even before the communications by Myers, Liszt, and Silver Birch, a spirit entity identifying himself as Johannes of Glastonbury, a monk who had lived from 1497 to 1533, communicated by means of automatic writing a number of messages to Frederick Bligh Bond, the director of excavations at Glastonbury Abbey, concerning the layout of the abbey grounds in his day. Johannes alluded to a group soul when it was suggested by another spirit entity that Johannes might be "earthbound" and his recollection colored somewhat by "clinging to vanished dreams." In fractured English, Johannes responded: "Why cling I to that which is not? It is I, and it is not I, butt parte of me which dwelleth in the past is bound to that which my carnal soul loved and called home these many years. Yet, I, Johannes, amm of many partes, and ye better parte doeth other things – Laus, Laus Deo – only that part which remembreth clingeth like memory to what it seeth yet." [5]

As noted in Chapter VI, when William Stainton Moses asked Imperator about reincarnation, he was told that only the most advanced Intelligences are able to discourse on that subject and that it is not given to the lower ranks of the spiritual hierarchy to know. "There are still mysteries, we are fain to confess, into which it is not well that man should penetrate," Imperator cautioned...What is wise and well will be done...There are other aspects of the question which, in the exercise of our discretion, we withhold; the time is not yet come for them. Spirits cannot be expected to know all abstruse mysteries, and those who profess to do so give the best proof of their falsity." [6]

In his 1939 book, *Reincarnation for Everyman*, Shaw Desmond states that there are two approaches to reincarnation – the "terrestrial" and the "celestial." The former view has the individual returning again and again as the same man, while the latter view has man "solely as *spirit* and his temporary inhabitancy of the physical body as but a tiny projection of the Greater Self, which is the real man."[7]

I came to realize that aforementioned mystics and spirit communicators may have been rejecting reincarnation in the terrestrial sense but not in the celestial. "Think of an atom," Liszt told Brown. "It is made up of protons and neutrons which all go to make up the nucleus surrounded by electrons. That is what a soul is like. These separate parts are held together in the nucleus, but the parts can be isolated. And it is the isolated parts of the nucleus of the soul so to speak which can manifest as various personalities in your world. These are what the reincarnationalist calls different incarnations – but they all belong to one soul which can choose which particular part of the soul it wishes to manifest."[8]

When Frederick Bligh Bond asked another of the Glastonbury spirits, a more fluent speaking one, about reincarnation, the spirit replied: "You understand not reincarnation, nor can we explain. What in you reincarnates, do you think? How can you find words? Blind gropers after immutable facts, which are not of your sphere of experience."[9]

Thus, I am content to look at reincarnation much like I look at God – beyond my comprehension.

[1] Brown, Rosemary, *Unfinished Symphonies*, William Morrow and Company., New York, 1971, p. 115

[2] Ballard, Stan A., and Green, Roger, *The Silver Birch Book of Questions & Answers*, Spiritual Truth Press, London, 1998, p. 190

[3] _____ p. 191

[4] Cummins, Geraldine, *The Road To Immortality*, The Aquarian Press, London, 1955, p.p. 62-63

[5] Bond, Frederick Bligh, *The Gate of Remembrance*, B. H. Blackwell, Oxford, 1918, p. 95

[6] Moses, William Stainton, *More Spirit Teachings*, Meilach.com, Sec. II, p. 6

[7] Desmond, Shaw, *Reincarnation for Everyman*, Andrew Dakers Ltd., London, 1939

[8] Brown, p. 117

[9] Bond, Frederick Bligh, *The Hill of Vision*, Constable & Co., Ltd., London, 1919, p. 9.

APPENDIX C

SUICIDE

There was a dramatic increase in the suicide rate during the Great Depression of the 1930s. If people who are losing their life savings in the current economic crisis are similarly inclined, they should reconsider. According to messages from the spirit world, they'll just take their problems with them.

While there is a certain amount of conflicting information coming through mediums, the discerning student of mediumship comes to understand that spirits are not all-knowing, that some know little, if anything, more than they did when incarnate, that some are devious and intend to mislead, and that for the well-intentioned spirit, explaining celestial matters in terrestrial terms can be extremely difficult. Moreover, messages are often unintentionally "colored" by the mind of the medium, or they can be misinterpreted by the medium.

However, suicide is one subject on which the spirit messages all seem to agree. While there may be some conflicting messages relative to suicide by terminally-ill people, the messages overwhelmingly condemn traditional suicide. They strongly suggest that the individual who hopes to escape from his or her problems here in the material world does not do so.

Communicating through Gladys Osborne Leonard*, a trance-voice medium, Claude Kelway-Bamber, a British pilot killed during World War I, told his mother that nothing can kill the soul. "You see, therefore, a suicide, far from escaping trouble, only goes from one form of misery to another; he cannot annihilate himself and pass to nothingness," Claude stated.[1]

In her 1964 book, *Post-Mortem Journal,* Jane Sherwood, an automatic writing medium, related information coming to her from a spirit known as "Scott," a pseudonym for a spirit later identified as Colonel T. E. Lawrence, aka "Lawrence of Arabia." Scott told of encountering one of his old friends in the afterlife, one who had killed himself. "He was in a kind of stupor and I was told that he might remain in this state for a long time and that nothing could be done about it," he penned through Sherwood's hand. "We watched over him and were loath to leave him in the misty half-region where he was found...Until he regained consciousness there he had to remain; had we forcibly removed him his poor body would not have been able to stand the conditions of our plane...Now and again I went back to find him still in the same quiet coma, and seeing the state of his astral form I almost dreaded his awakening."

Scott went on to say that such long-lasting comas are common with suicides. "It is really a merciful pause during which some of the damage to their emotional bodies is quietly made good." Scott and others attempted to help their old friend, but his condition was such that progress was slow.

"I am told that there is a belief that suicides remain in coma until the time when they would normally have died," Scott added. "This is one of those propositions which are impossible of proof, since no one can say when their hour would have struck had they not anticipated it. It is a fact that this state of coma lasts for varying periods, but there is also a long period of unconsciousness in many who have come by violent deaths. A suicide differs from such a one because his emotional state is usually far worse and takes much longer to clear, but a long period of coma may supervene on death in either case...Eventually he must awaken and take on the task of fitting himself to enter his own appropriate sphere of being. This is where he can be and is helped. There is often a long convalescence before he can get free of the sin and suffering of his violent end."[2]

Lilian Bailey, a renowned medium, also received messages about suicide. One spirit communicated through her that the suicide will have to live through that which his physical body would have had to endure. "He will see the whole thing happening. He will be consciously living with the same problems, although there will be no one condemning him and there will be beauty all around him."

The spirit went on to say that even though the suicide may feel he was justified in taking his own life, he is still a "gatecrasher" and that things are not ready for him in the spirit world. "It is very difficult to tell you how wrong it is. He can't go very far. He can only reach a certain 'half-way' stage. His dear ones may not be able to get to him — something like Berlin's Wall..."

Another spirit communicating through Bailey said: "It isn't what you've got, or whether you are blind, deaf or dumb, it's how you meet it. It isn't so much what you do; it's the motive you have for doing it." [3]

Red Cloud, the spirit guide of Estelle Roberts, one of England's great mediums, communicated that the person who commits suicide undergoes a premature birth into the spirit world. "He cannot immediately reach the plane of consciousness to which his evolution would entitle him had he fulfilled his allotted span on earth. Instead he remains suspended between the earth and the astral plane, which is the first stage beyond earth. In this state he is deprived, for the time being, of the company of his loved ones in the spirit world, unable to cross the barrier raised by his premature birth. Only when he has advanced in his evolution to the required degree can he rejoin those he knew and loved." [4]

For more than 40 years, Silver Birch (believed to be a pseudonym for a collective spirit group) spoke through the entranced Maurice Barbanell*. Frequently, members of the circle put questions to Silver Birch. When asked what the status of the suicide is in the spirit world, Silver Birch replied that he could not give an answer that applies to everyone. "It depends on the earthly life that has been lived," he said through Barbanell's vocal cords. "It depends upon the soul's progress; and, above all these things, it depends on the motive. The churches are wrong when they say that all suicide comes in the same category; it does not. While you have no right to terminate your earthly existence, there are undoubtedly in many cases, ameliorating factors, mitigating circumstances, to be considered. No soul is better off because it has terminated its earthly existence. But it does not automatically follow that every suicide is consigned for aeons of time into the darkest of the dark spheres." [5]

[1] Kelway-Bamber, L., *Claude's Book*, Psychic Book Club, London, p. 19

[2] Sherwood, Jane, *Post-Mortem Journal*, Neville Spearman, London, 1964, pp. 110-111.

[3] Aarons, Marjorie, *The Tapestry of Life*, Regency Press, London, 1991, p. 82

[4] Roberts, Estelle, *Fifty Years A Medium*, Transworld Publishers, Ltd., London, 1969, pp. 82-83

[5] Ballard, Stan A. & Green, Roger, *The Silver Birch Book of Questions & Answers*, Spiritual Truth Press, London, 1998, p. 213

APPENDIX D

RENOWNED RESEARCHERS & MEDIUMS
(cited in this book)

Maurice Barbanell (1902 – 1981) was a London journalist and a trance medium, most remembered as the medium for the entity known as **Silver Birch**. The son of Jewish parents, his father an atheist, Barbanell adopted his father's outlook during his younger years but later changed to agnosticism. While serving as secretary of a literary debating society, Barbanell listened to a speaker give a talk on Spiritualism. Very skeptical as to what the speaker had to say, Barbanell decided to investigate. At his second séance, he "fell asleep." When he awoke he was informed that he had been in a mediumistic trance and that an Indian spirit guide had spoken through him.

A home circle was formed and Silver Birch spoke regularly over the next 50 years, offering much wisdom. The proceedings were always recorded in shorthand. Sitters frequently put questions to Silver Birch and he answered questions on every conceivable subject, ranging from abortion through death, free will, love, reincarnation, transplants, and suicide, to zodiac. Indications were that Silver Birch was a pseudonym for a spiritually advanced soul who did not feel his actual name would lend to the validity of his messages. When asked about his true identity, he described himself as "a voice crying out in the wilderness," and said that his mission was to bring light to those struggling in the darkness.

Sir William Barrett (1844 – 1925) was a professor of physics at the Royal College of Science in Dublin and one of the pioneers of psychical research. It was Barrett's idea to form the Society for Psychical Research in London in 1882. In 1899, Barrett developed a silicon-iron alloy known as stalloy, used in the commercial development of the telephone and transformers, and also did pioneering research on entoptic vision, leading to the invention of the entoptiscope and a new optometer. He was a fellow of the Royal Society, Philosophical Society, Royal Society of Literature as well as a member of the Institute of Electrical Engineers and the Royal Irish Academy.

Barrett's book, *Death-Bed Visions*, first published in 1926, the year after his death, is still popular today. It offers a number of intriguing reports in which a dying person appears to see and recognize some deceased relative or friend, some of them involving instances where the dying person was unaware of the previous death of the spirit form he sees.

Several weeks after his death, Barrett's wife, Lady Florence Barrett, a prominent, obstetric surgeon and Dean of the London School of Medicine for Women, began receiving very evidential messages from Sir William through the mediumship of **Gladys Osborne Leonard**. Over the next eleven years, Lady Barrett sat with Leonard every few months, taking verbatim notes as Sir William communicated. She also received evidential messages from several other mediums. A book, *Personality Survives Death*, published in 1937, resulted from these sittings.

Geraldine Cummins (1890 – 1969) was a gifted automatic writing medium. She authored 22 books, 15 of them received by automatic writing, including several now considered classics in the field, viz., *The Spirits of Cleophas* (1928), *Beyond Human Personality* (1932), *The Road to Immortality* (1933), *Mind in Life and Death* (1956), and *Swan on a Black Sea* (1965). She also had abilities in the areas of psychometry and precognition.

Cummins was introduced to mediumship during 1914 when she met Hester (Dowden) Travers Smith in Paris and observed her receive messages from "alleged deceased persons" by means of the Ouija board. At the time, Cummins, although only 17, had already subscribed to the theory that it was all coming from the subconscious by a means of what was then referred to as cryptesthesia. However, she eventually came around to accept the spirit hypothesis. Cummins' dedication to mediumship actually began in 1923, after she met Beatrice Gibbes, a London resident and member of the Society for Psychical Research. Gibbes took her under wing and helped her develop as a medium. Over the next 25 years, Gibbes acted as Cummins' manager, arranging for sitters, keeping records, removing pages during the sittings, and checking on evidence. Cummins spent eight months of every year living with Gibbes in London, while the other four months of the year were spent in Dublin.

Gibbes described Cummins' condition during the automatic writing as semi-trance or light dream-state or sometimes in a deeper condition of trance. The handwriting almost always resembled that of the communicating entity when alive and did not resemble Cummins' own handwriting. Moreover the phraseology was much different than that used by Cummins in her conscious state. Much was offered in the way of evidence during personal sittings. *Beyond Human Personality* and *The Road to Immortality* were purportedly dictated by **Frederic W. H. Myers**, the pioneering psychical researcher who died in 1901. They contained much about the nature of the afterlife.

Andrew Jackson Davis (1826 – 1910), was a gifted American clairvoyant and magnetic healer who came to be called "the Poughkeepsie seer." In 1844, Davis had a strange experience in which he reportedly went into a semi-trance and found himself 40 miles from his home. During this journey, he claimed to have experienced a state of mental illumination after meeting Galen and **Swedenborg.** He soon began taking dictation from spirits while in a trance or magnetized state. His writings on spiritual matters resulting from his clairvoyance, including *The Great Harmonia*, are said to have influenced the metaphysics of both Spiritualism and of Christian Science.

When New York State outlawed the practice of spiritual healing in 1880, Davis entered medical school and obtained degrees in both medicine and anthropology so that he could continue to heal, often without payment.

Emily S. French (1831 – 1912) was a direct-voice medium through whom much apparent wisdom was communicated. She was investigated primarily by Edward C. Randall, a prominent Buffalo trail lawyer, who sat with her more than 700 times over a 20-year period and wrote several books about her mediumship.

After satisfying himself that Mrs. French was a genuine medium and that he was hearing from "spirit people," including his mother and father, Randall began having Mrs. French sit in his (Randall's) home in order to rule out any kind of trickery. As she developed the voices turned from whispers to loud voices, the loudest one being that of her primary control, an American Indian known as Red Jacket. Randall pointed out that each voice had individuality and sometimes spoke in a foreign tongue. Randall further mentioned that the strength of the voices varied greatly, much as they do in earth life.

While many of the early messages were of the evidential type, Randall considered them a waste of time as he was more interested in the "new philosophy," including information on the meaning of life, the nature of the afterlife, spiritual evolution, and other higher truths. Thus, his books about Mrs. French are mostly devoid of the usual evidential messages documented by other researchers.

Randall wrote that in addition to Red Jacket, he was lectured by Channing, Beecher, Tallmadge, Ingersoll, Hough, Segoyewatha, and hundreds of others from the spirit world. He referred to them as "matchless oratory."

Allan Kardec (1804 – 1869) was a French educator and philosopher who began investigating mediums in 1854. His real name was Hippolyte Léon Dénizarth Rivail, but he adopted the *nom de plume* of Allan Kardec when he began writing about his findings.

Educated at Institute of Pestalozzi at Yverdun, he had intended to enter the legal profession, as had his father and grandfather, but he devoted himself to education. In 1830, at age 25, he began giving gratuitous lectures to the public on chemistry, physics, comparative anatomy, and astronomy. Under his given name, he authored a number of works aimed at improving education in the public school of France, including *A Plan for the Improvement of Public Instruction* (1828) and *A Classical Grammar of the French Tongue* (1831). Besides French, he was fluent in German, English, Dutch, Greek, and Latin.

A friend of Kardec's had two teen-aged daughters who were mediums. Most of the messages coming through the two young ladies, the Boudin sisters, Caroline, 16, and Julie, 14, were frivolous or mundane, but when Kardec was present the messages became serious and profound. When Kardec inquired as to the cause of the change in disposition, he was informed that "spirits of a much higher order than those who habitually communicated through the two young mediums" came expressly for him, and would continue to do so, in order to enable him to fulfill an important religious mission.

Among the enlightened spirits purportedly communicating with Kardec were John the Evangelist, St. Augustine, St. Vincent De Paul, St. Louis, Socrates, Plato, Fénélon, Franklin, and Swedenborg.

Kardec would meet with one or both of the mediums a couple of evenings every week and put questions to the spirits. The sessions with the Boudin sisters went on for nearly two years before Kardec decided to put the messages in book form. His spirit instructors sanctioned the publication and Kardec was told by them that he should adopt the name Allan Kardec. There are two theories as to the name: it was an old British name in his mother's family and it was his name in a past life. It may be that both are true.

The first publication of *The Spirits' Book* contained only information gleaned from the spirits communicating through the two sisters, but a revised edition, the one remaining in circulation, includes messages from other spirits through other mediums.

Kardec called the philosophy coming from the spirits *Spiritism.* While the body of knowledge Kardec was developing was similar to what in England and the United States was developing as *Spiritualism,* Spiritism was more unified, and, unlike much of Spiritualism, embraced reincarnation. Its basic tenet is that we are immortals souls continually evolving through higher and higher realms of existence.

Kardec continued communicating with spirits until his death at age 64. He also wrote, *Christian Spiritism, The Gospel – Explained by the Spiritist Doctrine, The Medium's Book* (also called *The Book on Mediums*), *Heaven and Hell,* and *Genesis.*

Gladys Osborne Leonard (1882 – 1968) is considered one of the greatest trance mediums in the annals of psychical research. While **Leonora Piper** was referred to by Professor William James as his "white crow" – the one who proved that not all crows are black, Mrs. Leonard, whose career began near the time that Piper's was ending, was referred to as "England's white crow" and the "British Mrs. Piper." Some of the very best evidence for the survival of consciousness came through her mediumship.

Leonard's mediumship began to unfold in December 1910, after she was married and working as a stage actress. With two friends, Florence and Nellie, Leonard began experimenting with the table-tilting method of spirit communication. After 26 failures, they received messages from several people, including Leonard's mother. These messages were spelled out by the table tilting, so many times for each letter of the alphabet. During this first successful sitting, a long name was spelled out, beginning with "F." As they could not pronounce it, they asked if they could abbreviate it by drawing several letters from it. The communicating entity consented and the three women selected "F-E-D-A" as the name for the entity.

Leonard and her two friends continued sitting at the table night after night, receiving messages from deceased friends and relatives as Feda acted as a kind of spiritual mistress of the ceremonies. Over the next several years, Leonard progressed from table tilting to trance mediumship, as well as automatic writing and occasionally the direct-voice. Early in 1914, Feda told Mrs. Leonard that she must become a professional medium and prepare for something big and terrible, apparently World War I. Leonard was reluctant to charge for her services, but when Feda pointed out that ministers and doctors are paid for their services, Leonard gave in to the suggestion.

Leonard gained worldwide fame from the publication of Sir **Oliver Lodge's** 1916 book, *Raymond or Life and Death,* which reported on many evidential messages Lodge received from his son Raymond, who had been killed on the battlefield the prior year. During a three month period in 1918, Leonard was exclusively engaged by the Society for Psychical Research, which had 70 of their researchers sit anonymously with her. The overall report was that good evidence of surviving personality had been obtained and that there was no trickery or fraud of any kind involved with Leonard.

In addition to her autobiography, *My Life in Two Worlds,* published in 1931, Leonard authored *The Last Crossing* (1937) and *Brief Darkness* (1942).

Sir Oliver Lodge (1851 – 1940) was a professor of physics and mathematics before becoming principal of Birmingham University. He was knighted in 1902 for his scientific accomplishment, especially for his work in electricity, thermo-electricity, and thermal-conductivity. He perfected a radio wave detector known as a "coherer" and was the first person to transmit a radio signal, a year before Marconi. He later developed the Lodge spark plug. He joined the Society for Psychical Research soon after its formation in 1882 and investigated many cases of mediumship, including those of Leonora Piper, **Gladys Osborne Leonard**, and Eusapia Paladino. Through his investigations, he came to accept the reality of mediumship and to believe in the survival of consciousness at death. Much to the dismay of many of his materialistic colleagues in science, Lodge made his beliefs public.

In spite of his high standing in the scientific community, Lodge continually suffered from attacks by scientists grounded in materialism, but he refused to abandon his convictions and interest in psychical research, authoring a number of books on the subject.

William Stainton Moses (1839 – 1892) was an ordained clergyman of the Church of England, a pioneering psychical researcher, and a gifted medium. He is most remembered for the latter, producing both physical and mental phenomena.

After taking his Master's degree at Oxford in 1863 and being ordained as a clergyman, he served as a curate on the Isle of Man for some five years, before returning to London, where he was appointed English Master in University College, a position he would hold until 1889.

Initially, Moses frowned upon mediumship, calling the mediumship of D.D. Home, the renowned Scottish-American physical medium. the "dreariest twaddle" he had ever come across. However, during a sitting, on April 2, 1872, Moses received some very evidential information about a friend who had died. After a number of other sittings with mediums, Moses became convinced that he was indeed communicating with the spirit world, and soon thereafter he began to realize that he was a medium himself. A small circle of friends gathered regularly to observe and record the phenomena coming through him, including levitations luminous hands, a great variety of communicating raps, numerous lights, direct writing (no hand holding the pencil), apports, the passage of matter through matter, the direct voice, and trance voice, the latter including inspirational messages given by various spirits through the entranced Moses.

While different spirits came through, the chief communicator called himself **Imperator**, a pseudonym. Imperator added that spirits named Rector and Doctor were his immediate assistants. He had come, he said, to explain the spirit world, how it is controlled, and the way in which information is conveyed to humans.

On March 30, 1873, spirit messages started coming through Moses' hand by means of "automatic writing." This method was adopted, Moses was informed, for convenience purposes and so that he could preserve a connected body of teaching. Those teachings were compiled in two books, *Spirit Teachings,* published by Moses in 1883, and *More Spirit Teachings,* collected and published after his death in 1892.

Frederic W. H. Myers (1843 – 1901) was a classical lecturer at Trinity College, Cambridge before becoming one of the founders of the Society for Psychical Research in 1882. He is sometimes referred to as the "father of psychical research." His book, *Human Personality and Its Survival of Bodily Death,* published in 1903, two years after his death, is considered a seminal work in the field. Harvard professor William James referred to Myers as the pioneer who planted the flag of genuine science upon psychical research. " University of Geneva psychology professor Theodor Flournoy opined that Myers name should be joined to those of Copernicus and Darwin, completing "the triad of geniuses" who have most profoundly revolutionized scientific thought.

Although not educated as a psychologist, Myers has been credited with developing a systematic conception of the subliminal self as well as a theory holding that telepathy is one of the basic laws of life. In fact, it was Myers who coined the word "telepathy," previously called "thought transference." According to Dr. Sherwood Eddy, a distinguished American writer of the first half of the last century, Myers began to explore the subconscious, or subliminal self, simultaneous with and independently of Freud. While Freud accepted atomic materialism, seeing philosophy as a mere rationalization and religion as outright fraud, Myers concluded that the Power behind the universe is superorganic, in a higher category to which human personality belongs. He saw psychical research as a meeting place of religion, philosophy and science. Since materialism had, in the wake of Darwinism, become the *intelligent* approach, Myers' view did not gain widespread acceptance.

In *Human Personality,* Myers explored disintegrations of personality, genius, sleep, hypnotism, sensory automatism, phantasms of the dead, motor automatism, trance, possession, and ecstasy. Through his extensive scientific research, Myers original belief in survival of the consciousness at death was restored. His interest in psychical research apparently continued on after his death,, as he is credited with giving us perhaps the strongest evidence yet obtained for survival in the "cross correspondence" cases. In those famous cases, Myers is said to have provided fragments of information through four mediums in separate parts of the world – fragments which seemed meaningless and incoherent until pieced together. Communicating through **Geraldine Cummins**, Myers explained much about his new environment on the other side of the veil.

Leonora Piper (1859 – 1950) was probably the most celebrated and tested American medium ever, She was referred to by Professor William James of Harvard University as his "white crow," the one who proved that all crows are not black.

Piper discovered her mediumship ability, which was initially of the trance voice type, in 1884 while sitting with a psychic healer. She lost consciousness and a young Indian girl named Chlorine began speaking through her. As her mediumship developed, a spirit calling himself Phinuit, who claimed to have been a French physician when alive, became her primary control, relaying messages from his side through Mrs. Piper to those sitting with her.

Piper was "discovered" by Professor James after his mother-in-law informed him of a very evidential reading she had had with Piper. Highly skeptical, James sat with Mrs. Piper and was stunned by the accuracy of the facts given to him about deceased relatives. In 1887, James, who had been persuaded by Professor **William Barrett** of England to form an American branch of the Society for Psychical Research (ASPR), turned over the study of Mrs. Piper to Dr. Richard Hodgson, an Australian who had been teaching in England. Hodgson moved to Boston to become executive secretary of the ASPR. He studied Piper for some 18 years, sitting with her an average three times a week, until his death in 1905. After his death in 1905, Hodgson began communicating through Mrs. Piper, adding to the evidence.

William T. Stead (1849 - 1912) was a dedicated journalist, author, social reformer, and pacifist, who was on his way to New York to give a speech on world peace at Carnegie Hall when he became a victim of the *Titanic*. He is remembered in psychic circles as the founder of *Borderland*, a quarterly journal devoted to psychical subjects, and as founder of Julia's Bureau, a psychic bureau intended to demonstrate the reality of survival after death as well as to assist in a spiritual revival.

In 1909, three years before his death, he published *Letters from Julia*, a series of messages purportedly coming to him through automatic writing from Julia T. Ames, an American newspaperwoman.

Soon after his death, Stead began communicating through various mediums. According to Rev. Charles L. Tweedale, the Church of England vicar of Weston, Stead appeared at a sitting given by Etta Wriedt in New York on April 17, three days after his death. In attendance were Vice-Admiral W. Usborne Moore and Estelle Stead, Stead's daughter. Moore reported that Stead talked with his daughter for at least 40 minutes. He described it as the most painful but most realistic and convincing conversation he had heard during his investigations of mediumship. General Sir Alfred E. Turner reported that he held a small and private sitting at his home with Mrs. Wriedt when Stead began talking. There was no question, Turner stated, that the voice was Stead's. At a later sitting with Wriedt, Turner saw Stead materialize, wearing his usual attire.

Dr. John S. King, a Toronto physician and president of the Canadian Society Psychical Research, reported receiving over 70 messages from Stead, the first one coming within two days of the Titanic disaster. They came through several mediums, including Mrs. Wriedt. In 1917, shortly after being discharged from the army, Pardoe Woodman began receiving messages from William T. Stead by means of automatic writing. Estelle Stead then started sitting with Woodman and receiving both evidential facts as well as information about her father's transition and new life.

Emanuel Swedenborg (1688 – 1772) was a scientist, inventor, statesman, author, and mystic. Considered one of the world's greatest polymaths, he is credited with making significant discoveries in astronomy, anatomy, magnetism, mechanics, chemistry, and geology. Fluent in nine languages, he was also an accomplished musician and horticulturist. When Stanford University researchers attempted to calculate the IQ of history's greatest minds by applying the Terman Standard Intelligence Test to a massive database of historical scholars, Swedenborg, Johann Wolfgang von Goethe, and John Stuart Mill finished in a virtual tie for first place.

At the age of 55, Swedenborg had a series of paranormal experiences which led him to abandon his scientific work and pursue spiritual studies through clairvoyance and/or out-of-body experiences. The last 27 years of his life were devoted to these spiritual explorations, resulting in volumes of books reporting on his other-worldly adventures.

After the advent of Spiritualism in 1848, Swedenborg is said to have appeared to **Andrew Jackson Davis** and contributed to his enlightenment and to have communicated with **Allan Kardec**. He also communicated much about the afterlife through the mediumship of Dr. George T. Dexter. **William Stainton Moses** was informed by spirit communicators that Swedenborg and Benjamin Franklin, working together, figured out how to communicate with the earth realm, thus giving rise to the communicating raps and table levitations that kicked off the Spiritualism epidemic in 1848.

BIBLIOGRAPHY

Aarons, Marjorie, *The Tapestry of Life*, Psychic Press, Ltd., London, 1979

Bailey, Alice A., *Death: The Great Adventure*, Lucis Press Ltd., London, 1985

Ballard, Stan A. & Green, Roger, *The Silver Birch Book of Questions & Answers*, Spiritual Truth Press, London, 1998

Barrett, Sir William, *On the Threshold of the Unseen*, E.F. Dutton & Co., New York, 1917

Barrett, Sir William Barrett, *Death-Bed Visions*, third edition, The Aquarian Press, Northamptonshire, England, 1986 (originally published in 1926)

Barrett, Lady Florence, *Personality Survives Death*, Longmans, Green and Co., London, 1937

Beard, Paul, *Living On*, Continuum, New York, 1981

Becker, Ernest, *The Denial of Death*, Simon & Schuster, NY, 1973

Beichler, *James E., To Die For*, Trafford Publishing, Victoria, B.C., 2008

Berger, Arthur S. and Joyce, *The Encyclopedia of Parapsychology and Psychical Research*, Paragon House, 1991

Bond, Frederick Bligh, *The Gate of Remembrance*, B. H. Blackwell, Oxford, 1918

Bond, Frederick Bligh, *The Hill of Vision*, Constable & Co., Ltd., London, 1919

Borgia, Anthony, *Here and Hereafter*, H. G. White, San Francisco, 1968 Burton, Jean, *Heyday of a Wizard: Daniel Home, The Medium*, Alfred A Knopf, New York, 1944

Cameron, Margaret, *The Seven Purposes*, Harper & Brothers, New York & London, 1918

✓ Cayce, Edgar, *No Death: God's Other Door*, A. R. E. Press, Virginia Beach, VA, 1998

Chambers, John, *Conversations with Eternity: The Forgotten Masterpiece of Victor Hugh*, New Paradigm Books, Boca Raton, FL, 1998

Cooke, Aileen H., *Out of the Mouth of Babes*, James Clarke & Co., Ltd., London, 1968

Crookall, Robert, *The Supreme Adventure*, James Clarke & Co., Ltd., Cambridge, 1961

✓ Crookall, Robert, *Out of Body Experiences*, Carol Publishing Group., New York, NY., 1970

Crookes, Sir William, *Researches into the Phenomena of Modern Spiritualism*, Austin Publishing Co., Los Angeles, Calif., 1922 (fourth edition of 1906 book)

Cummins, Geraldine, *The Road to Immortality*, The Aquarian Publishing Co., London, 1932

Cummins, Geraldine, *Unseen Adventures*, Rider and Company, London, 1951

Cummins, Geraldine, *Mind in Life and Death,* The Aquarian Press, London, 1956

Cummins, Geraldine, *They Survive,* Psychic Book Club, London, no date

Davis, Andrew Jackson, *Death and the After Life,* Colby and Rich, Boston, 1865

De Brath, Stanley, *Psychical Research Science and Religion,* Methuen & Co., London, 1925

De Morgan, Sophia Elizabeth, *From Matter to Spirit,* Longman, Green Longman, Roberts & Green, London, 1863

Doyle, Arthur Conan, *The Vital Message,* George H. Doran Company, New York, 1919

Doyle, Arthur Conan, M.D., LL.D., *The History of Spiritualism,* George H. Doran Company, New York, 1926

Doyle, Arthur Conan, *Pheneas Speaks,* George H. Doran Co., New York, 1927

Duffey, Mrs. E. B., *Heaven Revised,* Two Worlds Publishing Co., Manchester, UK, 1921

Eddy, Sherwood, *You Will Survive Death,* The Omega Press, Surrey, England, 1954

Edmonds, I. G., *D. D. Home: The Man Who Talked with Ghosts,* Thomas Nelson Inc., Nashville/New York, 1978

Edmonds, John W., and Dexter, George T., *Spiritualism,* Partridge & Brittan, New York, 1853

Farr, Sidney Saylor, *What Tom Sawyer Learned from Dying,* Hampton Roads Publishing Co., Ltd., Norfolk, VA, 1993

Fenwick, Peter & Elizabeth, *The Art of Dying,* Continuum, New York, NY, 2008

Findlay, Arthur, *The Psychic Stream*, Psychic Press Ltd., London, 1939

Flammarion, Camille, *Death and Its Mystery: Before Death*, T. Fisher Unwin, Ltd., London, 1922

Ford, Sarah Louise, *Interwoven*, The Progressive Thinker Publishing House, Chicago, 1907

Fortune, Dion, *Glastonbury*, The Aquarian Press, Northamptonshire, England, 1986

Funk, Isaac K., *The Widow's Mite and Other Psychic Phenomena*, Funk and Wagnalls, New York, 1911

Garland, Hamlin, *Forty Years of Psychic Research*, The MacMillan Co., New York, 1936

Garland, Hamlin, *The Mystery of the Buried Crosses*, E. P. Dutton and Company, New York, 1939

Garrett, Eileen J. *Awareness*, Creative Age Press, Inc., New York, NY, 1943

Gilbert, Alice, *Philip in the Spheres*, The Aquarian Press, London, 1952

Greaves, Helen, *The Challenging Light*, Neville Spearman, Suffolk, UK, 1984

Greber, Johannes, *Communication with The Spirit World of God*, Johannes Greber Memorial Foundation, Teaneck, NJ, 1979

Hamilton, Trevor, *Immortal Longings*, Imprint-Academic.com, Exeter,UK, 2009

Hardinge, Emma, *Modern American Spiritualism*, University Books, New Hyde Park, NY, 1970 (reprint of 1869 book)

Hare, Robert, M.D., *Experimental Investigation of the Spirit Manifestations*, Partridge & Brittan, New York, 1855

Harris, Louie, *They Walked Among Us,* Psychic Press Ltd., London, 1980

Heagerty, N. Riley, *The French Revelation,* Morris Publishing, 2000

Hegy, Reginald, *A Witness Through the Centuries,* E. P. Dutton & Co., Inc. New York, NY, 1935

Holt, Henry, *On the Cosmic Relations,* Houghton Mifflin Company, Boston and New York, 1914

Home, Daniel D., *Incidents in My Life,* University Books, Inc., Secaucus, N.J.,(no publication date given, but reprint of an 1862 book)

Hyslop, James H., *Contact with the Other World,* The Century Co., New York, 1919

James, William, *The Varieties of Religious Experience,* 1902

Johnson, Raynor C., *Nurslings of Immortality,* Harper & Brothers, New York, 1957

Josephson, Matthew, *Victor Hugo,* Doubleday, Doran & Co., Inc., Garden City, New York, 1942

Jung, C. G., *Memories, Dreams, Reflections,* Vintage Books, NY, 1961

Kardec, Allan, *The Spirits' Book,* Amapse Society, Mexico, reprint from 1857

Kardec, Allan, *The Book on Mediums,* Samuel Weiser, Inc., York Beach, Maine (reprint of 1874 book)

Kenawell, William W., *The Quest at Glastonbury,* Garrett Publications, New York, 1965

Kelway-Bamber, L., *Claude's Book,* Psychic Book Club, London, originally published in 1919

Kierkegaard, S., *Fear and Trembling,* Doubleday & Co., Garden City, NY, 1954

Kubler-Ross, Elisabeth, *On Life After Death*, Celestial Arts, Berkeley, Calif.

Laubscher, B. J. F., *Beyond Life's Curtain*, Neville Spearman, Jersey, C.I., 1967

Leonard, Gladys Osborne, *My Life in Two Worlds*, Cassell & Company, Ltd., London, 1931

Leonard, Gladys Osborne, *The Last Crossing*, Psychic Book Club, London, 1937

Litvag, Irving, *Singer in the Shadows*, The MacMillan Co., New York, NY, 1972

Lodge, Oliver, *The Survival of Man*, Moffat, Yard and Co., New York, 1909

Lodge, Sir Oliver, *Raymond or Life and Death*, George H. Doran Company, New York, NY, 1916

Lodge, Oliver, *Past Years*, Charles Scribner's Sons, New York, 1932

✓ Long, Jeffrey, *Evidence of the Afterlife*, Harper-Collins, New York, NY, 2010

Martinez, Susan B., *The Psychic Life of Abraham Lincoln*, New Page Books, Franklin Lakes, NJ., 2007

McEneaney, Bonnie, *Messages*, Harper Collins Books, New York, 2010

Medhurst, R. G., *Crookes and the Spirit World*, Taplinger Publishing Co., New York, NY 1972

Moody, Raymond, *Glimpses of Eternity*, Guideposts, New York, NY, 2010

✓ Morey, Robert A., *Death and the Afterlife*, Bethany House Publishers, Minneapolis, MN, 1984

Moses, William Stainton, *Spirit Teachings*, Arno Press, New York,1976, reprinted from 1924 edition published by London Spiritualist Alliance

Moses, William Stainton, *More Spirit Teachings*, Meilach.com

Myers, F. W. H., *Human Personality and its Survival of Bodily Death*, University Books, Inc., New Hyde Park, NY, 1961 (reprint of 1903 book)

Naylor, William, *Silver Birch Anthology*, Spiritualist Press, London, 1955

Ortzen, Tony, *The Seed of Truth*, The Spiritual Truth Press, Surrey, UK, 1987

Osis, Karlis and Haraldsson, Erlendur, *At the Hour of Death*, Avon Books, New York, 1977

✓ Owen, G. Vale, *The Life Beyond The Veil*, George H. Doran Co., New York, 1921

Paget, Fanny Ruthven, *How I Know That the Dead are Alive*, Plenty Publishing Co., Washington, D.C., 1917

Perry, Michael, *Psychical and Spiritual*, The Churches' Fellowship for Psychical and Spiritual Studies, Lincolnshire, 2002

✓ Peters, Madison C., D.D., *After Death What?* The Christian Herald, 1908

Pole, Wellesley Tudor, *Private Dowding*, Pilgrims Book Service, Norwich, England, 1917

Prince, Walter Franklin, *The Case of Patience Worth*, University Books, New Hyde Park, NY., 1964 (original from Boston Society for Psychic Research, 1927)

Rinpoche, Sogyal, *The Tibetan Book of Living and Dying*, Harper, San Francisco,1994

Riva, Pam, *Light from Silver Birch*, The Spiritual Truth Press, Surrey, UK, 1983

Robbins, Anne Manning, *Both Sides of the Veil*, Sherman, French & Co., Boston, 1909

Roberts, Estelle, *Fifty Years a Medium*, Gorgi Books, London, 1959

Roberts, Jane, *The Afterdeath Journal of an American Philosopher*, Prentice-Hall, Inc., Englewood Cliffs, NJ, 1978

Rosher. Grace. *Beyond the Horizon*, James Clarke & Co., London, 1961

Rosher, Grace, *The Traveller's Return*, Psychic Press, Ltd., London, 1968

Savage, Minot J., *Life Beyond Death*, G.P. Putnam's Sons, New York, NY, 1900

Scott, John, *As One Ghost to Another*, Spiritualist Press Ltd., London, 1948

Sculthorp, Frederick C., *Excursions to the Spirit World*, The Greater World Assoc., London, 1961

Sherwood, Jane, *Post-Mortem Journal*, Neville Spearman, London, 1964

Sherwood, Jane, *The Country Beyond*, Neville Spearman, London, 1969

Smith, Eleanor Touhey, *Psychic People*, William Morrow & Co., Inc., New York, 1968

Smith, Susy, *The Book of James*, G. P. Putnam's Sons, New York, 1974

Smith, Suzy, *The Afterlife Codes*, Hampton Roads, Charlottesville, VA, 2000

Spong, John Shelby, *Rescuing the Bible from Fundamentalism,* HarperCollins Publishers, New York, NY, 1991

Stead, William T., *After Death or Letters from Julia,* The Progressive Thinker Publishing House, 1909, (reprinted by Kessinger Publishing, LLC)

Stead, Estelle, *The Blue Island,* Hutchinson & Co., London, 1922

Stevens, J. Gay, *The Girl with the Golden Hair,* FATE Magazine, Dec. 1972, Jan. 1973

Storm, Stella, *Philosophy of Silver Birch,* Psychic Press, London, 1969

Swain, Jasper, *On the Death of my Son,* Turnstone Press, 1974

Thomas, Charles Drayton, *Life Beyond Death with Evidence,* W. Collins Sons. & Co., Glasgow, 1928

Thomas, Charles Drayton, *Some New Evidence for Human Survival,* Spiritualist Press Ltd., London, 1922, (Revised 1948, no copyright)

Travers Smith, Hester, *Voices from the Void,* E. P. Dutton & Company, New York, 1919

Tweedale, Charles L., *Man's Survival After Death,* Psychic Book Club, London, 1925

Twigg, Ena, *Ena Twigg: Medium,* Hawthorne Books, Inc., New York, 1972

Wallace, Alfred Russel, *Miracles and Modern Spiritualism,* George Redway, London, 1896

Wehner, George, *A Curious Life,* Horace Liveright, New York, 1929

Wetzel, Joseph, *The Bridge Over the River,* Anthroposophic Press, 1974

White, Steward Edward, *Across the Unknown,* Ariel Press, Columbus, OH, 1987

White, Stewart Edward, *The Unobstructed Universe*, E. P. Dutton & Co., New York, 1940

Whiting, Lilian, *The Spiritual Significance*, Little, Brown, & Co., Boston, 1901

Wickland, Carl A., *Thirty Years Among the Dead*, Newcastle Publishing co., Inc., 1974 (original publication in 1924)

Wickland, Carl A., *The Gateway of Understanding*, National Psychological Institute, Inc., Los Angeles, 1934

Wood, Frederic H , *Through the Psychic Door*, Psychic Book Club, London, 1954

Zammit, Victor, *A Lawyer Presents the Case for the Afterlife*, Ganmell Pty Ltd., Sydney, NSW Australia, 2002

Paperbacks also available from
White Crow Books

Marcus Aurelius—*Meditations*
ISBN 978-1-907355-20-2

Elsa Barker—*Letters from
a Living Dead Man*
ISBN 978-1-907355-83-7

Elsa Barker—*War Letters
from the Living Dead Man*
ISBN 978-1-907355-85-1

Elsa Barker—*Last Letters
from the Living Dead Man*
ISBN 978-1-907355-87-5

Richard Maurice Bucke—
Cosmic Consciousness
ISBN 978-1-907355-10-3

G. K. Chesterton—*The
Everlasting Man*
ISBN 978-1-907355-03-5

G. K. Chesterton—*Heretics*
ISBN 978-1-907355-02-8

G. K. Chesterton—*Orthodoxy*
ISBN 978-1-907355-01-1

Arthur Conan Doyle—*The
Edge of the Unknown*
ISBN 978-1-907355-14-1

Arthur Conan Doyle—
The New Revelation
ISBN 978-1-907355-12-7

Arthur Conan Doyle—
The Vital Message
ISBN 978-1-907355-13-4

Arthur Conan Doyle with
Simon Parke—*Conversations
with Arthur Conan Doyle*
ISBN 978-1-907355-80-6

Leon Denis with Arthur Conan
Doyle—*The Mystery of Joan of Arc*
ISBN 978-1-907355-17-2

The Earl of Dunraven—*Experiences
in Spiritualism with D. D. Home*
ISBN 978-1-907355-93-6

Meister Eckhart with Simon Parke—
Conversations with Meister Eckhart
ISBN 978-1-907355-18-9

Kahlil Gibran—*The Forerunner*
ISBN 978-1-907355-06-6

Kahlil Gibran—*The Madman*
ISBN 978-1-907355-05-9

Kahlil Gibran—*The Prophet*
ISBN 978-1-907355-04-2

Kahlil Gibran—*Sand and Foam*
ISBN 978-1-907355-07-3

Kahlil Gibran—*Jesus the Son of Man*
ISBN 978-1-907355-08-0

Kahlil Gibran—*Spiritual World*
ISBN 978-1-907355-09-7

Hermann Hesse—*Siddhartha*
ISBN 978-1-907355-31-8

D. D. Home—*Incidents
in my Life Part 1*
ISBN 978-1-907355-15-8

Mme. Dunglas Home; edited,
with an Introduction, by Sir
Arthur Conan Doyle—*D. D.
Home: His Life and Mission*
ISBN 978-1-907355-16-5

Edward C. Randall—
Frontiers of the Afterlife
ISBN 978-1-907355-30-1

Lucius Annaeus Seneca—
On Benefits
ISBN 978-1-907355-19-6

Rebecca Ruter Springer—*Intra
Muros: My Dream of Heaven*
ISBN 978-1-907355-11-0

CPSIA information can be obtained at www.ICGtesting.com
Printed in the USA
LVOW061812130312

272905LV00007B/49/P